Forest Dwellers, Forest Protectors: Indigenous Models for International Development

Richard Reed
Trinity University

Allyn and Bacon
Boston • London • Toronto • Sydney • Tokyo • Singapore

Vice President, Social Science: Sean W. Wakely
Series Editor: Sylvia Shepard
Series Editorial Assistant: Erika Stuart
Marketing Manager: Karon Bowers
Cover Designer: Jenny Hart
Electronic Composition: Siobhan Curran

ISBN: 0-205-19822-8

Printed in the United States of America

10 9 8 7 6 5 4   01 00 99

THE CULTURAL SURVIVAL SERIES IN ETHNICITY AND CHANGE

Allyn & Bacon

Series Editors, David Maybury-Lewis and Theodore MacDonald, Jr.
Cultural Survival Inc., Harvard University

Indigenous Peoples, Ethnic Groups, and the State, by David Maybury Lewis

Malaysia and the "Original People": A Case Study of the Impact of Development on Indigenous Peoples, by Robert Knox Dentan et al.

Forest Dwellers, Forest Protectors: Indigenous Models for International Development, by Richard Reed

Contents

Contemporary Development and
Guaraní Communities...77

Indigenous Models for
Sustainable Development.......................................119

Foreword to the Series

Cultural Survival is an organization founded in 1972 to defend the human rights of indigenous peoples, who are those, like the Indians of the Americas, who have been dominated and marginalized by peoples different from themselves. Since the states that claim jurisdiction over indigenous peoples consider them aliens and inferiors, they are among the world's most underprivileged minorities, facing a constant threat of physical extermination and cultural annihilation. This is no small matter, for indigenous peoples make up approximately five percent of the world's population. Most of them wish to become successful ethnic minorities, meaning that they be permitted to maintain their own traditions even though they are out of the mainstream in the countries where they live. Indigenous peoples hope therefore for multi-ethnic states that will tolerate diversity in their midst. In this their cause is the cause of ethnic minorities worldwide and is one of the major issues of our times, for the vast majority of states in the world are multi-ethnic. The question is whether they are able to recognize and live peaceably with ethnic differences, or whether they will treat them as an endless source of conflict.

Cultural Survival works to promote multi-ethnic solutions to otherwise conflictive situations. It sponsors research, advocacy and publications which examine situations of ethnic conflict, especially (but not exclusively) as they affect indigenous peoples and suggests solutions for them. It also provides technical and legal assistance to indigenous peoples and organizations.

This series of monographs entitled "The Cultural Surviv-al Series on Ethnicity and Change" is published in collabora-tion with Allyn and Bacon (the Simon and Schuster Education Group). It will focus on problems of ethnicity in the modern world and how they affect the interrelations be-tween indigenous peoples, ethnic groups and the state.

The studies will focus on the situations of ethnic minori-ties and of indigenous peoples, who are a special kind of eth-nic minority, as they try to defend their rights, their resources and their ways of life within modern states. Some of the vol-umes in the series will deal with general themes, such as eth-nic conflict, indigenous rights, socio-economic development or multiculturalism. These volumes will contain brief case studies to illustrate their general arguments. Meanwhile the series as a whole plans to publish a larger number of books that deal in depth with specific cases. It is our conviction that good case studies are essential for a better understanding of issues that arouse such passion in the world to-day and this series will provide them. Its emphasis nevertheless will be on relating the particular to the general in the comparative con-texts of national or international affairs.

The books in the series will be short, averaging 100 pages in length, and written in a clear and accessible style aimed at students and the general reader. They are intended to clarify issues that are often obscure or misunderstood and that are not treated succinctly elsewhere. It is our hope therefore that they will also prove useful as reference works for scholars and policy makers.

David Maybury-Lewis
Theodore MacDonald
Cultural Survival, Inc.
46 Brattle Street
Cambridge, Massachusetts 02138
(617) 441-5400 fax: (617) 441-5417

Acknowledgments

Despite the long hours alone in the field or office, research and writing is inevitably a group process. I would like to thank those family, friends and colleagues who assisted me in this project. Ruth Knutson deserves appreciation for giving me use of her computer and milkhouse to write this manuscript. Sylvia Shepard and Kathy Barrientos helped enormously in converting it into a book. I would also like to recognize Myrtle Juelg and the students in my economic anthropology class for their helpful comments and suggestions. Finally, my greatest thanks are to Avarijú, Kai Taní and the other Guaraní who accepted me into their lives and taught me what I know about life in the forest. I hope they approve of the lessons that I have learned.

Introduction

THE GUARANÍ OF THE FOREST

The Guaraní of Paraguay and Brazil occupy one of the largest remaining subtropical forests of the new world. In the shade of the trees' high canopy, they fit our stereotypes of indigenous peoples. The Guaraní are small, bronze-skinned and prefer to wear a minimum of clothing. Their communities are set in forest clearings, connected with one another by footpaths through the dense underbrush. Houses are small, with thatched roofs and few furnishings. Social groups are led by old men wearing feather headdresses; people who use their religious knowledge to counsel the group.

The Guaraní differ from our images of indigenous people in one very important aspect. They have not been isolated in their deep forests. In fact, the Guaraní have been in contact with the larger world since the 16th century, when the early Spanish explorers became their allies. Conquistadors took their wives from among the Guaraní women, and explored the region alongside the Guaraní men. Jesuit and Franciscan missionaries trekked through the territory and built churches in the forest for the Guaraní to worship in.

International economies invaded the South American forests long ago and drew the indigenous people into the world system. In the 19th century, merchants came into the forests of the Guaraní looking for timber, skins, oils and tea for the rest of the world. Rather than resist this expansion of the commercial system, the Guaraní entered it with enthusiasm. They collected goods from the forest to sell and purchased goods such as machetes and salt in return.

Commerce with the larger world has not destroyed the Guaraní. They have not been assimilated into Paraguayan or Brazilian society. As Europeans carved South America into nation-states, the Guaraní maintained their communities in the dense forests. Even as the descendants of the Europeans came to predominate in the region, Guaraní retained their indigenous religious, kinship and political systems.

Guaraní production has been the key to their ethnic survival. Although they entered the international commodity market, they refused to abandon their traditional subsistence production. While they worked for cash, the Guaraní continued to produce their own food in gardens and collect it in the forest. They have had access to soap and axes, clothes and sunglasses, but they also have produced the corn and venison they need to eat. With subsistence assured outside the commercial sector, the Guaraní have maintained their communities and social systems. Kin connections continue to be the primary network for establishing a home, appointing leadership, and organizing religious ceremonies. In sum, the Guaraní have adapted the larger system to their own purposes; they have become linked to it without giving up their traditional social, economic and ecological systems.

After centuries of contact with the larger world, the relationship between the Guaraní and the larger society is threatened. In the last ten years, new kinds of production have moved into the forests of eastern Paraguay. Population growth and international investment are opening the area to intense colonization and development. In eastern Paraguay, cattle ranching and mono-crop agriculture are replacing the traditional economy of timber, skins, oil and tea. The forests are being felled and the new farmers are using soils for pasture, tobacco, cotton and soybeans. Since 1970, almost 30 percent of Paraguay's forests have been lost to farming and ranching; giving the country the highest rate of deforestation in Latin America.

As entrepreneurs buy and clear the forests, Guaraní are forced onto small reservations. On these small reserves, sometimes only a tenth of their previous area, they do not have the extensive forests they need for hunting, gathering and shifting agriculture. As Guaraní are forced to abandon their traditional production systems, they lose control of their relationship with the larger society. Traditional residence patterns, kinship systems, religious beliefs and political institutions are giving way to the authoritarian and hierarchical relations of the larger society.

Recent development not only destroys the existing forest and indigenous societies, it also devastates the soil and water. Land clearing ravages the very resources that support the new forms of development. Declining profits force farmers and ranchers to abandon their land and clear new fields in the forest.

The Guaraní can teach us new and better ways of using the forest. Guaraní forest residents manage the forest with great care. They earn a profit while protecting the resources they use, and have sustained this commercial development over centuries. This book describes Guaraní production systems and suggests them as an alternate model for using the forest. Preserving the forest not only protects indigenous people, but allows the continued economic development that all depend on.

GUARANÍ DEMOGRAPHICS

Most of the indigenous people in the lowlands of South America's southern cone belong to a series of related groups called the *Tupi-Guaraní.* Local groups speak related, although distinct, languages. In addition, these distinct groups have social similarities in the ways they organize kinship, residence, religion and politics.

This work focuses on the Guaraní who live in the forests of Brazil and Paraguay. Most of the population, about 15,000, has settled in eastern Paraguay. Anthropologists divide these Paraguayan Guaraní into 3 sub-groups: the *Chiripá*, the *Paitavyterā*, and the *Mbyá*. Although these groups differ in some aspects of language and culture, they are very similar in most respects. The Pai-tavyterã reside in the north, the Chiripá in the central, and the Mbyá in the southern forests near the Brazilian border.

The Guaraní live in 114 communities, which range from hamlets of three or four houses, called *Tapyi*, to large settlements of over a hundred families. Nuclear families occupy individual houses, which are clustered along paths that meander through the forest. They cut gardens into the forest that surrounds their houselots. Kinship connections tie households into larger communities; young couples build their houses near those of their parents. As a result, most households in a community are connected by ties between siblings or cousins.

Most of the Guaraní in eastern Paraguay are settled on small plots of land that are reserved for them by the national government. Since 1976, the Paraguayan government has been attempting to guarantee land to all indigenous communities in Paraguay. Almost 90 percent of the recognized communities have title to at least some land. Although not enough, as we will see below, reservations provide a modicum of security for the Guaraní of Paraguay.

A fourth indigenous group, the *Aché*, inhabit the forests of eastern Paraguay. The Aché are distinct from the Guaraní in physique, language, and culture. They forage for subsistence, rather than garden, and differ from the Guaraní in their relation to the larger society. Consequently, the Aché are not considered in this book.

The final important ethnic group of eastern Paraguay is made up of descendants of Europeans who migrated into the area. Europeans intermarried with the Guaraní of the region, producing descendants called *mestizos* or *criollos*. Today, this group makes up most of the population of rural Paraguay. Over the centuries, they have come to form a group with a strong sense of ethnic identity, neither indigenous nor European, but Paraguayan. They speak the Guaraní language and live and eat much as the Guaraní do, yet they are Catholic and have a firm allegiance to the Paraguayan nation.

The indigenous Guaraní of eastern Paraguay have not been isolated from these mestizos, but have learned to live in their midst. The Guaraní have accommodated the national system without sacrificing their economic independence or ethnic autonomy. As forests are cleared, however, the Guaraní are having increasing difficulty defending themselves and their culture from the larger society.

GEOGRAPHY

Eastern Paraguay is geographically diverse. As a traveler moves eastward, the low, flat wetlands along the Paraguay River slowly give way to high forested hills. The region lies on the western escarpment of the Paraná Plateau, a raised area that extends east to the Atlantic River. Erosion of the western flank of the Paraná Plateau has created a series of low hills along Paraguay's eastern border with Brazil. These *sierras* have Guaraní names: Mbaracayú, San Joaquín, and Amambay.

Eastern Paraguay is just south of the Tropic of Capricorn, about 25 degrees below the equator. The distance from the equator gives the region clear seasons. Rainfall cycles in a single annual pattern, between February highs and July lows, amounting to an average of fifteen to seventeen hundred millimeters each year. Temperatures climb to forty degrees centigrade for a few days in February and drop to freezing in July. Weather is generally moderate, usually ranging between sixteen and thirty degrees centigrade. Temperature variation throughout most days varies more than the seasonal changes.

The Paraná Plateau is drained by a network of streams and rivers that flow south to Buenos Aires and the Atlantic Ocean. Watersheds are separated from one another by low hills. The waterways start as babbling brooks in the highlands and work their way downhill, eventually flowing into the broad and meandering Paraná and Paraguay Rivers.

High canopied forests cover the Paraná Plateau, made up of hardwoods such as *lapacho* (*Tabebuia ipe*) and *cedro* (*Cedrela tubiflora*). The overstory shelters thick growth on the forest floor, a tangle of underbrush and vines that makes it difficult to walk through the forest. Low scrub forest grows along the region's many streams and rivers, where the high canopy is broken by dense growths of coco palms (*Cocos romanzoffiani*) and bamboos. As one moves off the high plateau toward the Paraguay River, the topography becomes lower and flatter and the high forests give way to marshy grasslands.

History

When Europeans arrived in South America, over a million Guaraní and related groups dominated the region from the Andes to the Atlantic Ocean. They were a massive and diverse ethnic group. Over the centuries, the group size and geographic region has greatly diminished. Nevertheless, the Guaraní continue to be an important ethnic group in the forests of eastern Paraguay.

Even before the arrival of Europeans in their midst, the Guaraní were changing and developing. Archaeologists believe that the Guaraní previously lived along the Amazon River. They cultivated manioc (*Manihot esculenta*), a starchy tuber that grows well in the thin soils of the rain forest. About a millennium ago, however, the Guaraní began a process of technical innovation that led to a massive migration throughout the forests of southern South America. First, they began to produce corn and beans, probably imported from the Andes. This provided better nutrition, but demanded more fertile soils than the rain forest could provide. The Guaraní were forced to seek better land on the high plains south of the Amazon River. As the Guaraní moved south, they discovered an environment that was abundant in new resources. Even as they continued to cultivate gardens, they harvested game, and managed the growth of useful trees in the forests. The Guaraní model of production can be best described as *agroforestry*. Agroforestry refers to any production system that integrates tree crops with cash crops, food crops, and animal raising (Clay 1988:32). Agroforestry uses forests, rather than replacing them with single crop agriculture or pasture. It builds on the existing system, managing its diversity to maximize the productivity.

With the benefits of these technical innovations, the Guaraní population grew dramatically. They were forced to colonize larger areas south of the Amazon floodplain to feed their expanding population. Thus, technical innovation and population growth led to a demographic expansion that carried the Guaraní throughout the southern cone. They migrated south onto the Paraná Plateau, east to the ocean, and up the Atlantic coast to the continent's eastern-most regions. These migrations forced them into the lands of other ethnic groups, and the Guaraní were forced to fight for the territory they occupied. Thus, the Guaraní preceded the Spanish as the bloodthirsty fighters and brutal colonists of South America's southern cone.

The arrival of the Spanish in 1537 integrated directly into the Guaraní expansion. In the decades before the arrival of the Spanish, the Guaraní were trying to expand into the foothills of the Andes. Between 1400 and 1430, emissaries of the Guaraní trekked across the hot, dry chaco lowlands to contact the Andean outposts of the Inca empire. On one hand, the Guaraní were interested in settling the fertile foothills of the Andes. On the other, the Guaraní were interested in commerce. By the time the Spanish arrived, the Guaraní had established trade routes from the Andes to the Paraná Plateau. They already had access to gold and silver from Inca mines.

When Sebastian Cabot (1476?-1557) first sailed south along South America's Atlantic coast, he met a boat loaded with gold and silver coming down the region's major river. The vision of easy wealth attracted him up the river, which he suitably called the Rio de la Plata ("River of Silver"). When he entered the region we now call Paraguay, he encountered a population of Guaraní of what seemed like several hundred thousand. Guaraní villages filled the forests and powerful political leaders could assemble armies of thousands of soldiers.

The Guaraní welcomed the first conquistadors. They needed military alliances to carve trading routes to the Andes, and the Spanish gratefully accepted local support in this large and unexplored area. The alliances were sealed as conquistadors set up households with Guaraní women, establishing a kin relationship with their new allies. The isolation of their newfound land helped create a distinct national identity very early. Conquistadors took Guaraní women as consorts and Guaraní men as allies. They also adopted the Guaraní language and diet. The first generation of mestizos born to these men maintained a strong and proud identification with both their European and Guaraní ancestors.

The Spanish and their Guaraní compatriots reached the Andes in 1546, only to find that Pizarro (1475-1541) had already conquered the Inca empire. Having lost the golden prize, they set out to get wealthy from the forests and residents of Rio de la Plata. These first conquistadors record the very comfortable life of the Guaraní. In 1541, the region's first governor, Cabeza de Vaca, traveled from the Atlantic overland to Asunción, passing through many Guaraní communities. He writes,

> They are . . . the richest people of all the land and province both for agriculture and stock raising. They rear plenty of fowl and geese and other birds; and have an abundance of game, such as boar, deer, and dantes (anta), partridge, quail and pheasants; and they have great fisheries in the river. They grow plenty of maize, potatoes, cassava, peanuts and many other fruits; and from the trees they collect a great deal of honey (1555/1891:118).

Unlike European society, which was organized around feudal power, the Guaraní were a fairly egalitarian society, linked to one another by kinship and religious ties. Hans Staden, a sailor captured by the Guaraní in 1550 reported, "I have seen no particular authority among them, except that by custom the young defer to the elders. They obey the orders of the chief of the hut; this they do of their own free will" (1557/1928:151). Extended families occupied large dwellings and acted as independent communities. Political leaders were able to bring dispersed groups together to migrate or make war, but they had no coercive power over their followers.

The forests of the Guaraní held no gold, but did have a native plant, called *yerba mate* (*Ilex paraguayensis*). The waxy, thick foliage of yerba mate harbors considerable caffeine. When the leaves are dried and pulverized, the caffeine is quickly released into infusions of hot or cold water. Guaraní collected yerba leaves to make a stimulating and pleasant drink. When drunk cold, called *tereré*, Guaraní added sweet and refreshing herbs, such as cilantro or mint. When steeped in boiling water, called *mate*, Guaraní added bark or leaves that had medicinal properties as astringents, purgatives or decongestants. The dawn air around Guaraní fires was filled with pungent aromas, as hot *mate* was passed between family members.

The conquistadors in the Andes sought yerba from the lowlands. They sought its stimulating effect as a tea to induce slaves to work harder in the mines and fields. As the tea gained popularity among both the conquistadors and the conquered, markets developed in Buenos Aires and Lima. The Spanish of Rio de la Plata first asked their Guaraní relatives to collect the yerba for shipment down river. That failing to satisfy their greed for wealth, the Spanish turned on their compatriots and forced them to collect the leaf. These labor drafts, called *encomiendas*, gave each conquistador rights to the labor of a specific group of Guaraní men. The Spanish set their laborers to work in the forests, collecting yerba mate, as well as honey and skins for the international market.

The Guaraní population declined precipitously after the conquest. Men were removed from their households and the birthrate dropped dramatically. Encomienda labor not only disrupted indigenous family life, it forced Guaraní to work under conditions that increased their susceptibility to disease. The Spanish brought new diseases, such as smallpox, measles, and even the common cold, to which the Guaraní were extremely vulnerable. Thus, one Guaraní leader complained to the governor in 1630 that,

> They have carried off our brothers, sons and sub-
> jects repeatedly to the Mbaracajú, where they are
> all dying and coming to an end... Those mate for-
> ests remain full of the bones of our sons and vas-
> sals, and our church is used only to bury the
> bones of our old women. Mbaracajú is the place
> where the poor little bones of our poor little vas-
> sals are piling up. We now have no more sons or
> vassals because of that Mbaracajú. It makes us
> sad. It means that we have no more houses or

plantations and it impoverishes and annihilates us. We no longer wish to go to Mbaracajú... (Hemming 1978: 258-259, translation by Hemming).

Missionaries sought to draw Guaraní out of the forests and into large religious communities, called *reducciones*, ostensibly to protect the Guaraní from the ravages of forced labor. Jesuits and Franciscans traveled up the rivers and established camps in the forest. While preaching the gospel in Guaraní, the missionaries themselves organized the Guaraní into labor gangs to collect yerba. By the 18th century, Jesuit yerba had an international reputation as the finest in the world. The Spanish and the missionaries eventually fought bitterly over the use of Guaraní labor. They each blamed the other for profiting from the work of the indigenous peoples.

The Guaraní of the forest were assaulted by a third force. Brazilian slavers arrived on the Rio de la Plata in the 17th century. These *bandeirantes* sought to take Guaraní from reducciones and encomiendas to work in sugar plantations on Brazil's northeast coast. Led off in chains, the vast majority of Guaraní died on the tortuous trek across thousands of miles to the plantations.

Forced labor drafts did not end until Paraguay won its freedom from Spain in 1812. By that time, a large portion of the Guaraní population had assimilated into the Paraguayan population. Guaraní left the encomiendas to settle in towns and worship at Catholic churches. These people came to comprise a Paraguayan nation, which differentiated itself from Argentina, Brazil and Bolivia based on its mixture of Guaraní and European roots. However, an important portion of the Guaraní remained in the forest. These Guaraní rejected the national society and continued to live a traditional lifestyle, protecting its uniquely Guaraní religion, kinship and political organization.

The Paraguayan economy continued to revolve around the production of yerba mate for the international market into the present century. Even as the gold played out in the mines in the highlands, the forests of Paraguay continued to produce goods for sale. The world demand for the tea grew and, by the turn of the 20th century, the forests of the Guaraní were among the richest resources on the continent. After the end of forced labor, yerba was collected by mestizo wage laborers. Large companies opened extensive marketing networks using a hierarchy of middlemen. These merchants bought yerba from the rural laborers in exchange for goods produced in the world manufacturing centers. The forests were soon filled with labor gangs who collected leaf and sent it down river to Buenos Aires, Lima, and Rio de Janeiro. Eventually, these corporations came to wield considerable power over affairs in both the national capitals and the isolated corners of the forest.

The indigenous people of the forest did not shun contact with this international economy. When the Spanish abolished encomiendas in 1812, the forest Guaraní sought opportunities to earn cash collecting yerba. The leaf that grew in their midst could be turned into cash. Thus, the Guaraní could buy salt from Bolivia and machetes made in England without having to leave their forest home. Even as the Guaraní collected yerba for the commercial market, they continued to produce subsistence goods for their own consumption. They integrated commercial production into indigenous economic activities, hunting, fishing and gardening.

It is important that commercial production integrated well with the other activities of the Guaraní. In labor demands, the cycles of harvesting in the yerbales did not conflict with the work of gardening or hunting. The activities exploited different ecological niches as well. The collection of leaves from trees used the forest, without degrading the environment that other Guaraní productive activities depended on.

Since 1970, there have been drastic changes in the forests of the Guaraní. As the population of Paraguay has grown and the national economy has expanded, new waves of settlers have carved out frontier towns in the forest. Colonization projects offer forested land to farmers at bargain prices, drawing people away from the heavily populated regions near the national capital. All-weather roads replace rivers as the primary means of transportation. These newcomers clear their gardens and build houses, shredding the forest canopy around their frontier settlements.

The economy of rural Paraguay has shifted dramatically since 1970 as well. Between 1970 and 1975, the national economy doubled in size. By 1989, almost a quarter (23.3 percent) of the country's commercial production derived from agriculture and ranching, primarily from soy, cotton and wheat (ECLA 1990:15). Commercial gathering has declined as intensive agriculture and ranching have become the driving forces in the national economy.

Paraguay's economic miracle was created by bringing new land under cultivation. Half the land in eastern Paraguay is arable and almost all areas are suitable for either ranching or farming. The Paraguayan government increased exports by quickly converting these forests to fields. Entrepreneurs and farmers clear land and sell the valuable timber to merchants who wend their way into the forest on muddy logging roads. The understory is burned in massive forest fires. Even before the ash cools, farmers plant the exposed soils in tracts of soybeans or pasture. These fields often extend over thousands of acres.

As their forests are turned into fields, Guaraní cannot continue agroforestry. First, traditional subsistence strategies become impossible. Without other land, the Guaraní are forced to recultivate their old gardens. They work harder to produce crops on the tired soils, with fewer returns. Game disappears with the forest. As food production becomes more difficult, the Guaraní are forced to purchase basic foodstuffs, such as corn and meat. Moreover, the Guaraní are losing the resources they need for traditional commercial gathering. As the need for cash increases, they have to find new ways to earn cash, a search that takes them from their communities and the forest. The Guaraní are moving into commercial agriculture. Like their Paraguayan counterpart, they are learning to grow tobacco, cotton, and soybeans to sell on the international market. This brings a host of new problems. The soils of eastern Paraguay are not deep. Within several years, crops need fertilizer, insecticide, and herbicide. Commercial agriculture is extremely capital intensive, leaving indigenous producers vulnerable to exploitation by merchants. New, powerful patrons control Guaraní access to production inputs, as well as access to the food indigenous families need until harvest.

Consequently, after four centuries of maintaining the social and cultural distinction from mestizos, the Guaraní are rapidly assimilating into the larger system.

LESSONS FROM THE GUARANÍ

The case of the Guaraní raises two important questions. First, how have the Guaraní survived over four centuries of contact with the national society and the international economy? Second, what is it about the new system that is disrupting the relationship between the Guaraní and that international system.

Regarding the first question, the following shows how the Guaraní adapted their traditional economy to the pressures and opportunities of that commercial system. Before the arrival of the Europeans in the new world, the Guaraní integrated hunting, fishing, gathering and gardening into a single complex subsistence system. This economy exploited many aspects of the ecosystem of the subtropical deciduous forests, yet did not exploit any one resource to the point of undermining the forest. The Guaraní production system both mimicked and shaped the local ecosystem. On one hand, Guaraní interplanted crops to imitate the diversity of the forest. On the other, Guaraní transformed the local ecosystem by managing the composition of fallow fields as they grew into standing forest.

The arrival of the Europeans brought new pressures and opportunities to the Guaraní. Besides the subsistence goods that the Guaraní gathered from the forest, they could now collect yerba, honey and skins for exchange. This placed new demands on the forest environment and for Guaraní labor. The Guaraní managed these new demands well, producing for exchange without destroying the balance between their economic systems and their environment.

Recently, however, intensive farming and ranching have disrupted the previous, stable relationship between the Guaraní and the larger system. Intensive use of a single resource, be it flora or soils, destroys the ecosystem. The destruction wreaked by contemporary development makes it impossible for the Guaraní to continue their diverse production systems. Destroying Guaraní economies, in turn, disrupts Guaraní relations with the larger society. Indigenous peoples are increasingly dependent on the larger society for subsistence, making them vulnerable to debt and manipulation by powerful patrons and markets.

The case of the Guaraní has implications for our more general understanding of indigenous peoples in relation to national societies and international economies. It is often assumed that indigenous groups are fragile. Indigenous culture and society are often portrayed as inflexible, unable to change or incorporate new elements. These perspectives suggest that indigenous groups have survived into the present only because they have been isolated from the pressures and opportunities of the larger world. The Guaraní, however, have been in contact with international forces for centuries. Not only were they exposed to other ways of thinking and organizing themselves, but they integrated new activities into their own economies. They did this without destroying their social organization or their cultural identity. Far from being isolated, these indigenous people struggled and won a place for themselves in the complex web of international relations.

The Guaraní can teach us a second important lesson as well. We need new models for economic use of these fragile ecosystems. The Guaraní economy provides this type of model. Their economy is a highly profitable system based on indigenous production patterns, which has protected the forest and earned a profit for producers for four hundred years. Perhaps we can use a similar strategy to assure that newcomers to the forest can be as successful.

THEORETICAL CONCEPTS

Agroforestry

Tropical forest areas are among the most diverse biosystems on earth. Over half the recorded species on earth have been recorded in tropical areas, and studies suggest that only 15 percent of the total species in these areas have been discovered. This diversity is both floral and faunal, and occurs in many micro-ecosystems in the forest. Agroforestry uses this diversity as a strength. It uses each area of the forest: the soils are farmed for their nutrient content, trees are exploited for their fruit and foliage, and animals are harvested or raised for the meat they produce.

Tropical systems are also fragile. Despite their verdant growth, the forests feed off a thin soil base. The forest canopy deflects the sunlight and the hard rains, providing a moist warm environment below. In this protection, plants grow profusely and, as they die, create a thin layer of rich detritus on the forest floor. These nutrients, in turn, feed the trees that form the canopy. Thus, the tropical forest is, in many ways a closed system. Nutrients move between living organisms and the soils, cycling vertically through the system under the protection of the forest cover.

Agroforestry builds off the ecosystem model of the rainforest. By incorporating tree crops into the production system, it preserves (or creates) the canopy and allows other plants and animals to flourish below. Crops that grow in the shade of the canopy mimic the understory of the original forest. In addition, agroforestry preserves the forests' diversity of plant and animal life. By having a variety of species coexisting, nutrients cycle among different plants and animals as they would in natural forests. In fact, agroforestry often increases ecological diversity. Small fields are sometimes opened for crops, ecologically similar to the small clearings created when a large tree falls in the forest. Many agroforesters allow the forest to reclaim these plots, creating small plots for sun-loving plants and animals to prosper.

Models of agroforestry vary in the control they exert over the environment. Some agroforesters clear the forest and replant it with commercial trees. In Costa Rica, for example, farmers have developed systems to intercrop bananas and coffee. The spreading fronds of the banana leaves protect the tender coffee from the most direct sunlight, yet give the low bushes room to flower and fruit. On the ground underneath, these farmers clear the soil and plant grass for cattle and food crops for themselves (Clay 1988:54).

In less managed agroforestry systems, the natural ecosystem is not dismantled. Domestic animals, food crops and valuable wild plants are nurtured within the existing system. Existing flora and fauna are harvested for cash and subsistence, and small gardens can be cut without damaging the standing forest.

Forest Management

Recent research in resource management suggests that indigenous groups have managed many tropical areas previously thought to be "natural." The Kayapo of Brazil plant and nurture food plants along their trails through the forest, then harvest these so-called "wild" plants on their treks. The Bora of eastern Peru have carefully culled plants in fallow fields to promote the growth of native species that they find especially valuable. This creates forest fields that have the appearance of virgin territory to the newcomer (Posey et al. 1984). As we learn the extent of these practices, we discover that human societies have carefully managed wide areas of the tropical environment.

Attention has focused recently on agroforestry methods in which natives commercialize forest resources without degrading the tropical environment (Redford and Padoch 1992). Clearly, both indigenous groups and forest settlers can benefit from mixed agroforestry. Producers can commercialize natural forest resources while fulfilling their subsistence needs by gardening, hunting and raising domestic animals.

Guaraní manage the forest through three primary activities: agriculture, hunting and gathering, and commercial tree cropping. Guaraní agriculture can be best described as shifting horticulture. Farmers fell small areas of forest and burn the debris, creating a layer of nutrient filled ash. Plants prosper in these soils for several years, after which declining fertility and spreading weeds force them to cut a new garden elsewhere. Rather than abandon an older field however, Guaraní replant with crops, such as banana or manioc, which need little care and survive on weak soils. Even as wild plants overtake the fallows, farmers continue to return to them periodically and harvest food from the dense regrowth. Thus, gardening builds into larger systems that affect the forest long after the forest has overtaken the plot.

The second important aspect of Guaraní agroforestry is hunting in the managed forests. Guaraní are careful not to overhunt game resources and usually spare young animals, but their management of game extends to a symbiotic relationship that farmers establish with game. Food attracts red brocket deer (*Mazama gouazoubira*), armadillos (*Dasypus novemcinctus*), pacas (*Cuniculus paca*) and peccaries (*Tayassu pecari* or *Tayassu tajacu*) into fields and fallows where they are shot or trapped. By sacrificing a small portion of their crops for animal invaders, farmers create an environment in which game populations grow. This allows hunters to provide meat to their families without decimating game populations. Guaraní manage fish populations as well. They capture fish in ox-bow lakes during annual floods, then harvest these fish ponds when gardens are bare and traps are empty. By protecting and promoting game populations, Guaraní have a predictable source of meat within close range. The third facet of Guaraní forest management involves commercial harvesting. The Guaraní collect a variety of materials for marketing into the national and international economies. Yerba mate is primary, but the Guaraní also extract oils from citrus foliage, hunt deer and peccary for skins, and cut timber for fence-posts. Rather than simply harvesting these materials, the Guaraní promote the growth of the trees and animals that they depend on. Yerba, citrus and other valuable trees are more common than if they were not important for the Guaraní economy.

In sum, Guaraní manage the forest to win both subsistence and a profit. Guaraní commercial agroforestry has allowed the forest residents to earn a profit without destroying the forest environment.

Sustainable Development

The management of forest through mixed-use strategies offers a model of sustainable development for newcomers to the forest. In conventional models, development has often been measured in per capita gross national product. However, the development models of indigenous peoples, such as the Guaraní, use more complex criteria. These models include attention to noncommercial, subsistence systems. Where conventional models measure success in terms of immediate profits, these models demand that the productive system sustain itself. Also, indigenous models of sustainable development include such human factors as health and nutritional status, educational achievement, access to resources and human rights (Pearce, Barbier and Markandya 1990:2).

Second, models of sustainable development are often based on no-growth economic systems. Conventional economic models assume growth and intensification as the standard mechanism for development. In these, economic health is measured by material accumulation and increasing consumption. Sustainability models, in contrast, distinguish between development and growth (Turner 1988). They suggest that households can satisfy needs without increasing production and consumption. Thus, at a larger level, the goal is not steadily climbing national output, but rather providing sufficient goods and services to the population.

GOING INTO THE FIELD

Anthropology sets itself apart from other disciplines through the experience of fieldwork. Living in a different society provides anthropologists the information they need to understand that specific culture and draw general conclusions about all human social groups. In the early years of this century, the anthropologist Bronislaw Malinowski left the comforts of his home and spent two years isolated from the world among the Trobriand Islanders. His immersion in Trobriand life provided a new, complex understanding of another culture and society. Few contemporary anthropologists are as isolated as Malinowski was, but total immersion in another society continues to be our primary research technique.

In my own research, I lived with the Guaraní for over two years. I worked, laughed, played, cried, sang and danced, and spent untold hours lounging around with the friends I made in Itanaramí. Being a part of family fights and political discord, as well as religious celebrations and fishing trips, taught me complexities of all facets of Guaraní life. When I returned to the United States, I shared my experiences with other anthropologists. Comparing Guaraní with other societies, I began to see similarities and differences. For example, young Guaraní men who hung around the community seemed very similar to the groups of bored young people hanging around American malls and bus stops. With these tentative generalizations, I began to outline more global statements about all human societies.

Fieldwork also taught me about myself and my culture. Seeing other people live such different lives challenged my basic assumptions about how people relate to one another. Watching the help Guaraní gave one another showed me the bond of trust that held Guaraní people together, ties that transcended the self-interested urges of each individual. Finally, as I'll explain below, seeing the American-made bulldozers push down the forest taught me much about the link between my life in the United States and the contemporary world of the Guaraní.

I had a more practical interest in the Guaraní as well. I went to Paraguay to study the demise of South America's indigenous people. As developers devastate lowland forests, international concern has focused on the genocide of native peoples. As a dictatorship with a reprehensible human rights policy, the Paraguayan government attracted considerable attention. The Paraguayan army was reported to be hunting the Guaraní and Aché, fencing them in paddocks, and letting them die in droves. These reports raised the specter of the Nazi doctor of death, Josef Mengele. He was reportedly at large in the forests of Paraguay, torturing the last of the indigenous populations (Arens 1976).

My initial visit to Paraguay made two things clear. First, the government had no explicit policy of war against the Guaraní. There were no concentration camps surrounded by barbed wire and no indication that Mengele had any contact with the Guaraní. On the other hand, even without a policy of genocide, the Guaraní were being wiped out. Loggers were clearing the forests and ranchers and agribusinesses were taking control of the land. Indigenous communities were taking refuge on these small islands of forest in seas of green fields. Trapped in these verdant prisons, residents were dispersing into nearby ranches and towns and assimilating into the poorest sectors of the larger society.

There was no need for the Paraguayan government to engage in genocide of the Guaraní. By simply ignoring the indigenous people they could allow a process called *ethnocide* to take place. That is, the Guaraní would disappear as a culture, their religion, political institutions and kinship systems would disappear, even without the destruction of them as biological entities. I changed my research plan to focus on the subtle and often complex forces that were destroying Guaraní society.

To understand the destruction of Guaraní society, it was necessary to work in communities that had not yet been overrun by the forces of development. Therefore, I decided to go to an isolated community and began my fieldwork before the process of intense change had begun. I took a bus to the end of the road, followed a jeep track for eleven hours and traipsed another hour on a narrow path through the forest. This took me into a.community called Itanaramí, beyond the reach of loggers' trucks and ranchers' fields. By working in communities that were about to confront the frontier of expanding agriculture and ranching, I could study the process of ethnocide from its beginnings.

With the help of a friend from the Peace Corps who spoke some Guaraní, I entered the community of Itanaramí to begin research. Explaining my purpose was not easy. Aware of the Guaraní fear of government officials, I was unaccompanied by political authorities. I was directed to the house of the religious leader, an older man called a *poraéa,* and explained that I was interested in learning about Guaraní culture. The small, wizened man listened calmly and then suggested that the community would meet and consider the idea. They would have a decision if I would return the following week. We walked out and took the two-day trip back to the capital city, with little to show for our long trek.

When I made the arduous trip back to the community, the leader reported that the group had not yet met. I again explained my interest in learning Guaraní culture and they asked me to return in a few days. After two more of these aborted entries, I realized that even if I were to explain its complexities, the Guaraní would not understand my work. The group was effectively avoiding a nonsensical dialogue. Nevertheless, my repeated trips showed the people of Itanaramí that I was not going to disappear and that I wasn't up to any immediate harm. On the third trip, the leader gave me permission to move into an abandoned schoolhouse in the community.

The first weeks in the community were lonely. Curious eyes followed me day and night and prying fingers explored every cranny of my small knapsack. I spoke little Guaraní and had no one to share my morning *mate* or long evenings with. Worse still, I became the object of the fascination of a group of adolescent boys. They hung out in my house, lounged in my hammock, explored my belongings, and generally made nuisances of themselves. The boys greeted my efforts to speak with peals of derisive laughter and quickly consumed the beans and rice that I cooked for myself. My first significant interaction with the Guaraní came when one of these young men stole my jackknife. This small, personal object had given me an inordinate amount of pleasure in those weeks and to lose it felt like a major calamity. When I reported the theft to the religious leader, he listened carefully but did not respond. I spent that night feeling very low, all alone in the forest with people who disliked me, and whom I distrusted. Much to my surprise, the next morning the old man stopped at my house with the knife. Months later I realized that the knife had probably passed through the entire community's hands during that short night. In any event, its return let me know that there was a caring group that I could establish some relationship with.

A second incident gave me a clue to the complexities of my situation. In my loneliness, I began drinking my morning *mate* with a family that lived across the path from my hovel. The household included a woman and her six children; her husband was nowhere to be seen. It was nice to be among children and warm myself by the early morning fire, even if real conversation was impossible. The social importance of this quiet morning ritual soon became apparent during a fishing trip with the young men. I was invited along to poison fish in a nearby ox-bow lake. (The task demanded many unskilled helpers whose sole task was to wade chest-deep into piranha and caiman infested water to spread poison -- they were glad to have me along.) As we jogged through the underbrush to the site, several of the young men began to joke and laugh. I quickly became aware that I was the focus of the mirth and, more slowly, realized that they were chiding me about sleeping with my single neighbor. When I dissented, they quickly and jokingly assured me that it was no problem, since most of them had slept with her as well!

I was mortified. This besmirched my reputation and put me in a category with the most reviled Paraguayan men, whose sole interest in Guaraní women was sexual. A bad reputation would raise impassable barriers between me and the rest of the community. After much argument, in bad Guaraní, I gave up the debate and was forced to suffer the humiliation of knowing that everybody was hearing the rumors. I returned to drinking *mate* alone.

Later I realized that linking me with my neighbor also worked to my benefit. First, the young men were including me in a rough masculine humor. Not as I would choose; but, they were including me as one of them. Secondly, the rumor made my presence less, rather than more, threatening to the community. By thinking I was paired with a woman who was sexually active throughout the community, the Guaraní saw me as less of a menace to other women. I stopped my vociferous denials and learned to be more careful in social appearances.

My ties to the community were strengthened by another neighbor, an old man named Kai Taní. He first befriended me, then took me in as his stepson, called *ra' anga*. The old fellow had recently lost his second wife to tuberculosis. Her adult daughter then abandoned a seriously retarded three year-old in his care. It was not a happy household. Worse yet, Kai Taní suffered from recurring tuberculosis that left him unable to work in his garden. Friends and relatives were his only source of food. Given our mutual unhappiness, and restricted from visiting my female neighbor, I often joined Kai Taní in the morning. I sipped *mate* with him, shared my food, and practiced my rudimentary Guaraní. He even chased off the gawking and bothersome young men.

When a family of nine abruptly joined me in my little house, I asked Kai Taní if I could hang my hammock under his roof. He assented. I brought my single bag and my hammock and moved in with him. Our friendship warmed around the fire and over many pots of beans and manioc. My relationship with Kai Taní and the community was formalized almost nine months later, in the annual name giving ceremony. During the initiation of young children, the religious leader discovered my Guaraní name and the forest aspect of my soul. Kai Taní sponsored me in the ritual, an action that solidified our relationship of fictive kinship and made me a formal member of the community.

Not only did I gain a stepfather, but I inherited a plethora of other relatives: cousins, uncles, aunts, nieces and nephews. I shared a new intimacy with all of them. They became more demanding of me, stretching my meager foodstuffs and emotional resources. On the other hand, they became more generous, sharing the goods from their traps and garden. In the end, these relatives taught me the most and it is to them I have the greatest debt. I can only hope that they feel I have in a small way repaid the favor.

FIELDWORK METHODS

As I struggled to get my personal life in order, I began to collect data concerning Guaraní society and culture. Even before I fully understood the Guaraní language, I began to participate in community activities. Since my interests were in the economic changes occurring in the Guaraní society, I sought out opportunities to hunt, fish, and garden with men. Besides the small amount of work I did, the Guaraní were willing to let me tag along for the entertainment of watching me struggle with an oversized machete. For me the activities were also fun. Work got me up from my hammock and out of my house, and I enjoyed walking through the forest, hunting, and fishing. This research technique, called participant observation, provided me with the insider's perspective of Guaraní work. It taught me things I never would have known otherwise. Sweating and straining with an axe gave me the experience of doing Guaraní work; my befuddlement and failures gave me answers to questions I never would have thought to ask.

As my language improved I began to interview individuals about Guaraní life. This provided me with information about areas of Guaraní knowledge that were more abstract. For example, talking with the Guaraní about the universe and their place in it gave me an understanding of Guaraní religion that participating in sacred ceremonies would never provide. Interviewing also allowed me to gather historical information. I was particularly interested in the economic history of the region, and talking with older residents provided a window into the past. I learned the work histories of the men and traced the movements of families among various communities. Being male, I did not learn about many aspects of the lives of Guaraní women. Indigenous society is not highly segregated, but Guaraní women were not comfortable being alone with me in the forest or gardens. I spent very little time participating in their work activities and I learned little about activities that were inherently female, like childbirth. Men were far more forthcoming about male activities than female.

Clearly, while my experiences provided a window into Guaraní life, they were very subjective. Interviews and participation in the community did not provide objective data about the Guaraní, nor was the information comprehensive. To compare the Guaraní with other societies, I needed more than individuals' opinions and reflections.

I used surveys to define Guaraní life in objective terms. One of my first tasks, then, was to do a census of Itanaramí and the surrounding communities to deduce the population size and general characteristics. To determine what work they did, I visited each person in the community each week at random times and noted their activities. This provided a picture of how the average person spent their day. In addition, surveying households over the course of a year defined the annual cycle of Guaraní work.

I used an economic survey to gauge the level and type of market involvement of the Guaraní, noting weekly income and expenditures for each household over an entire year. The task demanded that I be on friendly terms with each family, forcing me to visit each household almost daily. This was not entirely successful. Of the 23 households surveyed, my relations with several became strained, and I was forced to drop them from my survey pool.

To get information about the past, I went to the national archives in the capital city, which had records of past Guaraní communities and mestizo settlements in the region. This archival research led me to the handwritten records of Jesuit priests and colonial administrators, where I found the names and ages of the Guaraní workers requisitioned by the mestizo patrons. After weeks immersed in chaotic and vivid forest life, it was a relief to spend quiet days in dark reading rooms. Instead of scrambling after hunters along slippery forest paths, I sat in comfort and traced the history of the Guaraní through worm-eaten record books.

Anthropology seeks to describe society and culture in all its complexity. By using a variety of research techniques, it is possible to explore each of the different facets of Guaraní culture. The anthropologist analyzes kinship; economic and political institutions; indigenous culture and ideology; the past and present; in qualitative and quantitative terms. These various facets of indigenous culture and society fit together to provide a holistic understanding of Guaraní reality.

OVERVIEW OF THE BOOK

This chapter has explored Guaraní history, introduced some concepts needed to understand their present, and described my fieldwork. The next chapter analyzes Guaraní communities, describing how they integrate kinship, religion, leadership and economics in a single egalitarian system. The third chapter focuses on Guaraní production, analyzing how Guaraní agroforestry integrates gardening, foraging, and commercial collecting into a single, sustainable system. The fourth chapter analyzes recent development in Mbaracayú and details how colonists and agribusinesses are forcing Guaraní onto small reservations and destroying their economy. In the final chapter, this study suggests that the traditional Guaraní production system could be a model for ecologically sound, sustainable development by newcomers to the forest, not only here, but throughout the world.

2

Guaraní Social Organization

Itanaramí households are built along a dirt-covered forest path, which winds over gently rolling hills and across gurgling brooks under the shade of the high canopy. There is no obvious point at which you enter the community. Rather, the visitor spots an opening in the forest and abruptly comes upon a small clearing with a thatch roof shelter in the middle. As you pass that house, the forest closes again around the path. Farther along the path, over another small brook, you encounter another clearing and household. As you move through the community, you pass dozens of these households, but no central plazas or large buildings.

Some indigenous people of South America's lowland forests live in single large structures, where all members of the group's extended family share common living space. The Guaraní, in contrast, live in single family houses. A woman and man usually build a small thatch roof, roughly four meters by five meters square, that extends almost to the ground. They share this personal space with their children and, perhaps, an aging parent. The floor of the interior is packed with fresh red clay, and the yard is scraped clean of plants. A cooking fire is built in the middle of the house and men string their hammocks from the eaves around its periphery. Guaraní houses are invariably littered with children and dogs, and a pot of manioc is usually boiling on the fire.

Adults squat on carved logs and lean up against the roof supports, talking among themselves as they cook, sharpen machetes or rest.

Guaraní families value their privacy and each household's clearing is carefully isolated from neighbors by a wall of trees. Men cut their garden into the forest near a new home and, as soils deteriorate over the years, they cut new areas to plant. Houses are eventually surrounded by overgrown fields, called fallows, full of tall grasses, orange trees, banana plants, and the perennial manioc plants. Walking down a path in a Guaraní community, these fallows are often the first sign that one is approaching a house. The path opens from the cool freshness of the forest to the direct sunlight and the dry grasses of a family's field.

There seems to be little organization, or even connection, among these dispersed households. There is no bureaucracy to govern affairs, or leaders to mandate decisions. Despite the lack of formal organization, the visitor soon discovers that the households are closely tied and highly organized. Kinship, religious, political and economic networks integrate them into a cohesive unit with a single identity. Guaraní call these communities *tapyí*.

KINSHIP

How are tapyí organized, if there are no titles to land, no elected authorities, or no religious offices? First and foremost, Guaraní communities are defined by kinship relations. Ties between parents and children, siblings and cousins become the structure for allocating rights, responsibilities and authority. Villages usually include ten to twenty-five closely related households who join under the religious guidance of an older member of the community.

The Guaraní trace kinship through men and women. That is, they recognize as relatives all people with whom they share blood relations. This group, deriving from a progenitor in the distant past, is termed a *cognatic descent group*. As they include the descendants of a specific person, their size is determined by the number of generations one chooses to include. The descent group of oné's grandparent includes their cousins; the descent group of a person's great-grandparent, all his or her second-cousins; and that of their great-great grandparent, includes one's third-cousins. As the size of the group is logically infinite, a person determines its size for specific purposes.

Viewed from a progenitor, cognatic descent groups are clearly organized. From the perspective of an individual descendent, however, these relations are more complex. Guaraní marry outside their kin group, a practice called *exogamy*, and an individual is a member of their mother's kin group and their father's kin group. Since each parent is in turn a member of two descent groups, an individual's descent affiliations increase geometrically for each previous generation included. Thus, just as the size of each group is logically infinite, an individual has claim to innumerable descent groups on both sides of the family.

Guaraní do not determine social relations only through descent, but also through marriage ties. Guaraní households are linked to both of the family networks of the principal couple. Therefore, while cognatic descent groups are distinct, individuals and households are the nexuses of many different interlocking and interconnected relations.

You might wonder how people keep track and make sense out of these complex relationships. But kin relations do not exist in the abstract, they exist in use. Guaraní do not think in terms of kinship, but in rights and responsibilities that kinship relations give them. Guaraní activate kin networks to get things done. For example, kinship determines where a person can build a house and cut a field. An individual who is looking for a marriage partner will know to avoid close relatives. When moving into a strange area, a family will search out more distant relatives to provide them assistance. In short, all relatives are not important all the time, but all relations can be activated in specific situations for specific purposes.

A primary function of kinship is to determine who lives where. The houses that seem isolated and disparate are closely connected by familial relations. Just as households are made up of nuclear families, Guaraní residence groups are made up of extended kin groups. When a Guaraní girl leaves her house and walks to the garden, her path will probably pass the houses of her aunts, her uncles, and her grandpar-- ents. The children she sees playing at the stream most likely will be her siblings, cousins and maybe her nieces and nephews. In short, her everyday world consists of her relatives.

Since Guaraní are exogamous and live in close-knit groups of relatives, they must look elsewhere for marriage partners. Young women jump at the chance to join their parents at religious ceremonies in other tapyi; young men visit friends and relatives, ostensibly to look for work, but more commonly in search of love. Brief encounters are common and early pregnancies are not uncommon, but legitimacy is not of great concern among the Guaraní.

Eventually, young couples who are compatible and interested in establishing a family make a more permanent commitment. There is no formal ritual or public ceremony to mark the occasion of a marriage. Instead, setting up a household is the most public display of the relationship. A newly established couple is expected to live with the woman's parents. The new wife will pass her days as she had in the past, harvesting in the garden and cooking with her mother and sisters. A new husband is expected to assist his new wife's father in the garden and help her brothers fish, trap and collect in the forest. This bride service secures the young man's relationship with his wife. After a year of this bride service, and usually after a child is born, the newlyweds will move into a separate house a short distance from the first.

This *uxorilocal* residence, where women form the central core of the residence group, structures more extensive family networks. As several sisters marry, their parents' home is surrounded by their new households. Each couple will maintain a separate garden, but they usually work as a group and gather together for religious purposes. The original residence becomes the central node of a growing kin network, to which the sons-in-law are linked through their wives. The social group comprises the descendants of a group of women, expanding as women stay in the tapyi and men marry into groups of sisters.

The Guaraní tapyi, however, is not simply made up of groups of women. Just as women have the right to live near their parents, each man inherits the right to build a house and cut a garden in the forests of his parents. Therefore, as the parents of a group of married women die, and their own families grow, the bond between sisters is weakened. Couples often join the natal tapýi of the husband and, after years of separation, brothers rejoin one another in a male-centered residence group.

As the children of these groups mature and marry, residence rights become more extensive and diffuse. Individuals can make residence claims on the families of each of their grandparents. Most households can choose between three or four tapýi in which they have close relatives.

Kinship is important to rights to live in a particular area, but it does not determine what choices each family will make. With close ties to both the brothers of the husband and the sisters of the wife, a family is forced to choose which tapýi to live in. They make that decision on the basis of a variety of other reasons, looking for better garden soils, larger game populations, fewer mosquitoes and wage labor. In fact, it is not uncommon for established couples to move periodically between residence groups, shifting among several family groups where they have ties.

In sum, Guaraní descent rules do not create discrete groups, they create a series of overlapping networks for figuring residence. As a result, Guaraní tapýi are not single monolithic entities, but self-selected groups of close relatives, including brothers, sisters, uncles, aunts, cousins, parents, and children.

Guaraní Religion

Guaraní do not simply live in the forest, they consider themselves of the forest. This is clear in the name they call themselves Ca'aguyguá, or "People of the Forest." The forest relationship is more than a simple geographic marker, however, it has religious and cosmological significance as well. The Guaraní see themselves as originating from the forest and each person maintains a personal spiritual connection with it. Religious activity not only expresses this connection, it develops and strengthens the relationship.

Cosmology

Guaraní religion suggests that the world is a large flat land mass, called *Yvú*, thousands of miles across. Water surrounds this land, separating the mundane world from the supernatural realm. These ideas accurately portray the continent of South America, but with the feudal European idea that the edge of the world lies beyond the known oceans.

Guaraní cosmology is organized around an axis that runs from east to west, following the sun across the sky. The sun rises every morning from a heavenly realm known as *Yvymaräey, Land Without Evil*. In this idealized universe, there is neither sickness or hunger (Cadogan 1959:78). There are houses with wooden walls, windows, and picket fences; gardens teeming with tomatoes, lettuce and potatoes; and corrals filled with horses and cattle. (It is not coincidental that this realm is characterized by the goods of mestizo life.) After its daily trek across the sky, the sun sets each night in a sacred domain in the west. This celestial region, called *Ka'aruá*, is dominated by an enormous forest, which is filled with wild animals and fruits. In the center of this forest is an enormous throne, constructed of *ygary* trees (*Cedrela fisilis*).

The Guaraní recognize a variety of deities, but the primary god is called *Tupá* or *Ñanderuguazú*, meaning *Our Great Father*. The story of Tupá's arrival on earth is the principle Guaraní creation story. It reveals the importance of the forest, corn, and the division of labor in Guaraní life. Before there were humans on earth, Tupá came from the east, Yvymaräey, with his wife and a woven basket of corn. His wife, called *Jaryí* was pregnant with twins. He built a small home in the forest to protect them and planted corn in the fertile soil. After resting from his chores, Tupá demanded that his wife harvest the corn. She refused, pointing out that the crop could not mature in a matter of minutes. After a bitter argument over the corn, Tupá abandoned Jaryí and traveled west into the heavens where he now sits on his imperial throne.

Jaryí set out to follow Tupá, but soon lost the way. One of the twins called directions from her womb, which she followed in a vain attempt to catch up with her departing husband. Instead, she ends up in a den of a demonic jaguar and is taken captive. The trials and tribulations of Jaryí and the twins she bears provide a corpus of stories that explain much of the origin of things in the world. The twins Ñanderyke (*Our Older Brother*) and *Tyvyry* (*His Little Brother*), outwit the demons in a series of lively escapades and become important secondary deities in the Guaraní cosmology.

In the everyday world, Ñanderuguazú and Jaryí are represented by the sun and the moon. Although the Guaraní do not confuse the two in fact, they will often use the name for the celestial bodies (Kuaray and Jasy) interchangeably with those of the deities. The trajectory of the two celestial bodies provides a daily reminder of the deities and their trek out of the eastern Land Without Evil.

Ceremony and Community Relations

Guaraní religious activity revolves around singing, called *poraé*, in which the community communicates with the spiritual world. Chanting together links each person with the forest and reaffirms their ties with one another.

Each Guaraní has his or her own religious song, which they usually discover during a time of personal crisis or change. Songs come during sleep, when the soul is free to travel throughout the universe. The unfettered spirit communicates with the gods and learns from them. The knowledge is carried back to the waking world in monosyllabic intonations that often have little explicit meaning.

Chants are most often received in an archaic form of Guaraní or in a monosyllabic intonation that has no explicit meaning. People chant with a slow repetitious melody that develops a monotonous momentum of its own. The sounds and rhythm open a dialogue between the individual and the spiritual world. People appeal to god, Ñanderú, for guidance and support. In return, they receive knowledge of the supernatural, *marandú*, and the guiding principles for Guaraní life, called *teko marangatú*. Although everyone receives religious knowledge, some people feel called upon to share their power with the group. These *poraéa*, usually men, become the religious leaders of the community. They call their friends and family together to accompany them in chanting, to join in learning teko marangatú.

As dusk falls over a Guaraní tapýi, family groups wend their way through the darkening forest to the small fire that lights their leader's household. The leader stands in front of a small altar with several crosses decorated with carved birds and feathers. A small wick burns on the altar and throws yellow light on his face. He has decorated his head with a feathered band and crossed his chest with a woven bandolier.

Singing while facing east toward the place where the sun rises, the leader shakes a rapid cadence with his gourd rattle, called a *mbaraká*. Moved by the rhythm, he steps in time to the beat, marking the beat in a rolling back-and-forth movement. As the group gathers, men take up their own mbaraká and join the leader in his steady chanting. Women sit in a semicircle in the darkness, often cradling young children. They pound large bamboo logs against the ground, beating a deep, resonant cadence to accompany the chanting. The pulsating music fills the night air, and wanders into the surrounding forest.

Then, after completing this meditation, the religious leader will reveal his experience to the community. Breaking the magic of the dirge-like chanting, the poraéa will speak in conventional Guaraní to exhort his followers to treat one another correctly and counsels them to develop a relationship with the supernatural. He admonishes their failures, guides their decisions, and entreats them to work toward a state of divine grace.

The evening singing is part of monthly and annual ceremonial cycles. First, the monthly cycle of Guaraní religious activity peaks with an intense, prolonged chanting and dancing at the time of the full moon. Although leaders sing whenever they dream an important vision, the appearance of the full moon inspires the largest gatherings. Each month Guaraní communities sing, dance, and drink fermented corn, *kanguijý*, to the light of the rising lunar orb. These monthly kanguijyápe last several days. On the first day, the family of the religious leader will collect corn, chew it, then spit the mash into a long vat of water. The mash is allowed to ferment two days in the warmth of the sun, covered by banana leaves.

(Masticating the corn adds enzymes that promote fermentation.) As the corn ferments, the religious leader will sing each night, accompanied by his family.

On the evening of the third day, the night of the full moon, the number of congregants and the intensity of the singing increases. Beginning at dusk, the community will sing and dance, *jyrokyapy*. Several people may be moved to share their visions and visitors often come from neighboring tapyí. As the night progresses, the length of the chanting and the size of the crowd grows. People eventually fill the leader's small home and spill onto the cleared yard that surrounds the house. Parents build little fires and bundles of children fall asleep on the ground in the orange darkness.

The kanguijyápe reaches its peak with the rising of the moon. As the white orb emerges from the trees on the horizon, the entire group rises to its feet and joins the leader. The singing and instruments fill the night air. Then, at the end of long and intense chanting, the leader calls for the kanguijΔ. An assistant, called an *yvyraijá*, brings a bowl of the mash in a hollow gourd. Holding a lighted wick over the fluid, the poraéa proclaims the liquid ready to drink. Young people run to get gourds and rush to distribute kanguijý to their family and friends. Adults and children alike share the lightly alcoholic drink and the air is filled with celebration.

After the group has drunk its fill and rested awhile, young people often break into a rowdy line dance. This dance is more playful than sacred, and lets the adolescents frolic and flirt among themselves. The night ends in a swirl of dust and laughter, as the sacred space is filled with young people using their dance lines to play Crack The Whip, sending their smaller siblings rolling into the dirt.

Religious ceremony does more than provide celebration and guidance for the community. It also serves to reaffirm relations among the members of the tapyí. Bilateral kin relations link all members of the group, but provide no boundaries for the group identity. The evening religious ceremonies define the membership of the group and establish boundaries between this and other tapyí. All members of the social group are expected to attend. Attending the ceremony shows one's community affiliation, avoiding it declares one's separation from the group. By joining in song and drinking kanguijý together, the Guaraní define and reaffirm their existence as a corporate group.

Religious ceremony can also be used to exclude potential community members. In one case in Itanaramí, a family arrived in the tapýi and declared their intention to be members. They claimed residence rights through a grandmother who had lived in the region decades ago. However, the little band was mistrusted and disliked by the people of Itanaramí. They had been ostracized from their previous community when one of their sons had killed a man in a drunken brawl. By gathering to chant, but not notifying them, the religious leader of Itanaramí effectively declared them non-residents of the tapýi.

Religious activity has an annual cycle that peaks with the initiation of new members at harvest time, called the *mitamongaraií*. The ceremony begins with long and intense singing at the maturing of the new corn, and culminates with the welcoming of all new things, including children, into the world. Preparations often take weeks. Women collect corn and brew kanguijý. From the fields they bring beans, squash, and sweet potato to be welcomed into the world. From the forest, men gather honey to feed the leader, beeswax and caraguatá fiber (*Bromleia balansae*) for wicks, red *urukú* (*Bixa orellana*) to decorate the women, and feathers for dancers and the altar. Leaders invite other tapýi to come and share the festivities. The initiation demands the power of the most knowledgeable singers, and pains are taken to see that these older men make the long trek. The ceremony gains strength and momentum as relatives arrive from distant tapýi.

The central focus of the harvest ceremony is the initiation of babies into the group. The name *mitamongaraií*, derives from three separate Guaraní words: *mitá* meaning *child*; *mo* meaning *to make*; and *ngaraií* meaning *honored adult*. Initiation is actually a naming ceremony. The leader uses the vision quest to discover Guaraní sacred names. These personal names give individuals a place in the community, as well as establish them in the forest and cosmological order.

The Guaraní describe the soul as having two elements, one human (*ayvú*) and the other animal (*asyiguá*). The human soul inhabits the body soon after birth and is socialized as a Guaraní. The other aspect of the soul, that of the forest, comes in animal form. A child may inherit the soul of a jaguar, a butterfly or, as is often the case, a small colorful bird, such as the tanager. A child with the asyiguá of a spider monkey would be playful and mischievous; the soul of the jaguar would be solitary and brooding. Unlike the human soul, the animal soul is unchangeable, refusing socialization. Initiation rites identify the forest entity that constitutes the forest soul. The leader must contact this forest soul and make it known to all members of the community. This new name then is called the *téra ca'aguy*, the *forest name*.

In the final days of the mitamongaraií, the chanting and dancing increase in intensity. The older leaders through the night, taking turns to maintain growing momentum in their exhortations. When not singing, they replenish themselves with mead (fermented honey-water) and rest in their hammocks. As they drift in their hammocks, their souls make the journey to the sacred realm and receive the names of the initiates.

After several weeks of work and several nights of nonstop singing, the initiation reaches its crescendo. The most powerful of the leaders join forces and dance together. The dancers, each with a lighted wick in their hand, approach the young children in their mothers' arms. Then, blowing on the forehead of the child, the old man intones the téra ca'aguΔ of the infant, giving it a permanent presence in the community. Finally, the entire group gathers in a long line in front of the dancing ground. The leader then reinitiates each individual of the group. He sings in front of each, hands them a burning wick, and redivines their forest name.

While the evening chanting defines the members of the tapyí, the mitamongaraií creates a larger ethnic identity. All Guaraní have forest names, and all individuals who have forest names have a presence in the Guaraní world. Without a Guaraní name, the individual does not have a presence in Guaraní society. After I had lived with the Guaraní for almost a year, the religious leader, Avarijú, said it was time to divine my forest name. Supported by Kai Taní, I was initiated with the children in the following mitamongaraií. This gave me a formal and permanent tie with both the forest and the Guaraní. The power of the téra ca'aguy can be seen in its use in curing. When a Guaraní is near death, after all other remedies fail, the leader will often divine a new soul for patients. He gives them a new identity, which can live, even as the sickness destroys the person's previous identity.

Religious Migrations

Guaraní religion suggests that the world is headed toward a final destruction. Myths tell how the earth was destroyed in the distant past and, although recreated, exists only until its final cataclysm. However, with proper preparation and devotion, humans can forestall the end of the earth or be saved from it to enter *Yvymaraey*, the *Land Without Evil*, in the company of Ñanderyke.

These beliefs caused a series of famous migrations of the Guaraní in search of salvation. Most famous was nineteenth century pilgrimages of Apapokúva-Guaraní from sites north of Itanaramí (Nimuendaju 1978/1914). As colonists moved from urban areas into the Paraná Plateau, their need for land and forest conflicted with the resident Guaraní. Inter-ethnic violence was common throughout the century. To avoid the pressures and conflict, Guaraní religious leaders began a series of migrations, leading their kith and kin out of the Paraná River basin. In tortuous treks of over two thousand miles to the Atlantic Ocean, they hoped to be saved from the tribulations of the mundane world.

Nimuendaju documents waves of migrations from the region of Mbaracayú, north and east toward the Atlantic Ocean. Groups of up to several hundred Guaraní gathered around especially popular poraéa. These charismatic leaders, inspired by visions and dreams, predicted the final destruction of the earth. Inspired with song and religious dances, followers set out on foot in search of the heaven, Yvymaraey, where they would escape the earth's ultimate annihilation.

Instead of salvation, the migrants discovered even greater hardship. Hostile mestizos and government militia met the migrant bands and tried to halt their progress. Well meaning Brazilians convinced some pilgrims to settle in the forests of western Brazil. Other emigres followed footpaths through unfamiliar terrain and hostile territory to the Atlantic. When they arrived on the beaches, they prayed, danced, and waited to be lifted en masse into the heavenly realm, from which the sun rises each morning. In 1912, Nimuendaju met one of the last of these bands on the white beaches south of Sao Paulo. The dwindling group waited desperately for salvation, until Nimuendaju finally convinced the remnants to accept a small reservation inland.

GUARANÍ LEADERSHIP

Leadership in Guaraní communities is based in kinship. As an individual matures, he or she acquires a level of power over progeny. This power is legitimized and reaffirmed in religious activities, developing into a political position of considerable authority. This type of political influence, however, is distinct from the coercive power that characterizes offices in conventional political bureaucracies.

Relations between parents and child create an incipient hierarchy that lends itself to structured decision-making and action. In Guaraní society, where extended family live in close contact, this relation extends to their nieces and nephews. As time bestows a level of experience on older members, parents and aunts and uncles are in a position provide help and guidance to their progeny.

This kin leadership is legitimized through religion. As older members acquire religious knowledge (*marandú*), they gain a vehicle to legitimize their influence within the group (*teko marangatú*). Guaraní religious values emphasize mutual respect between individuals, whatever their age, gender or social position, and kin leaders are expected to exemplify and enforce attitudes of mutual respect. For example, during a fight with his wife, a young man of Itanaramí chased his wife out of their house, brandishing a burning branch. Many people saw the incident, but it seemed to go unnoticed. Some hours later, however, when the fury of the fight had passed, his father's brother joined him in his house. As the two sat by the fires and stared into the light, the older man described the domestic violence of Paraguayan mestizos. The behavior of the younger man was never mentioned, but the message was heard and accepted.

As kin leaders develop marandú, they develop reputations that extend beyond their immediate kin group. Where several tapyí occupy a small area, a single leader may lead the religious ritual for the entire group. In the region of Itanaramí, several leaders have considerable reputations as wise men and therefore have influence throughout the area's Guaraní population. For the older men with broader political aspirations, this type of reputation can develop into a position of more general leadership.

In the past, it is possible that Guaraní leaders commanded influence over large populations. The first conquistadors reported Guaraní leaders who could amass armies of thousands against the Inca. During the famous religious migrations of the nineteenth century, we have seen that some leaders developed large followings and convinced them to travel thousands of miles over difficult conditions. Today, few Guaraní leaders achieve this type of influence and are more likely to provide guidance for a small, tightly knit kin group.

Guaraní leadership depends on influence, rather than power. Unlike political leaders in highly centralized state systems, Guaraní leaders do not have the ability to force their will on others. There is no corporal punishment or police force to enforce leaders' decisions. There is no structure that can coerce submission of dissenters. Rather, leaders appeal to religious ideology and practice to manipulate their followers. The political freedom of Guaraní society is in part based on the generalized access to resources. As every Guaraní household has membership rights in several tapyí, families can leave a tapyí at any time and join one of several others. Unpopular leaders soon find their tapyí diminished as families move to more suitable groups elsewhere.

GUARANÍ ECONOMICS

Guaraní Families and Generalized Exchange

As in politics and religion, Guaraní economic relations are organized around an infrastructure of kinship. Goods and services flow along kin and religious ties, allowing households to get the things families need to survive. Economic networks are broad and diverse. First, Guaraní families practice free and uncalculated sharing with other households in their tapyí. Second, Guaraní households carry on reciprocal trading with people who are more distant in geography and kinship. Finally, Guaraní are integrated into market networks, selling commodities to mestizo merchants and purchasing manufactured goods from world markets.

Economic exchanges with the three different levels are not simply broad, they differ in fundamental ways. Close kin engage in a generalized pattern of gift giving; distant relatives trade goods and work of an equal value in balance exchanges; and Guaraní sell commodities to mestizo patrons in hopes of making a profit. In a sense, these three types of exchange occur in separate spheres, with different actors, meanings, and social contacts for each. The value of a kilo of rice, for example, would be fundamentally different in each of the three social spheres.

Most economic exchanges occur among Guaraní who are close relatives. When Avarijú leaves his house on a hunting trip, he usually stops briefly to visit the family of his wife's sister who lives near the path. Being early in the morning, he often arrives as his relatives are roasting corn or having a breakfast of boiled beans. Guaraní etiquette demands that anyone arriving during a meal be offered food and Avarijú will unabashedly accept a healthy portion. When finished, he will make small talk for a while, but continue on his way without a word of thanks.

Returning from his trap line that evening with a paca or peccary over his shoulder, Avarijú will retrace his steps to his relative's house. This time he will take his machete and, without much fuss, slice off a portion of the kill for his sister-in-law. She will take the portion as if it were expected and quietly hang the meat in the rafters for the next meal. Thus, with little attention, goods move quickly among Guaraní households.

Guaraní exchange almost any personal belongings among close relatives, including food, clothing, and tools. A man without an axe must borrow one to clear his field. Likewise, the hunter who owns a gun will find it in great demand by his less fortunate friends and relatives. Once, at the beseeching of a close friend, I gave him a bright red baseball cap that was my most prized personal possession. He wore it for several days, then gave in to the entreaties of his brother and passed it on. In the subsequent weeks I saw my hat travel around the community, worn successively by each adult male. Finally, after several months, I came across a young boy proudly balancing its tattered remains on his head. My hat had been well used.

Food is one of the primary goods shared among households. Guaraní harvest most goods in large quantities. Killing a peccary, or even a paca, provides more meat than a family can consume immediately. Although planting is staggered to assure that all crops do not mature simultaneously, corn, beans and rice need to be harvested in quantities that are too great for a single family to consume in a short period. Excess food is wasted. Meat rots quickly in the warmth of the forest and pests soon invade bags of corn and beans stored in the rafters. By sharing the abundance, families assure that all foods are put to good use.

In addition, sharing food evens out the abundances and shortages that characterize the food-getting process of the Guaraní. Even a dedicated hunter like Avarijú is only sometimes successful. Today, he left fresh meat for his sister-in-law's family. Tomorrow he may come home empty-handed, but find that his brother has left a leg of a deer at his house. Thus, although a hunter is successful only one day in three, exchange systems assure that his family will have meat or fish most days.

These food exchange systems also guarantee that houses have access to the diversity of goods produced. Each household selects its own crop mix. Some plant rice in the low and wet areas along streams, others choose to plant peanuts. Some families have large stands of bananas, others devote themselves to tending stands of orange trees in the forest. The relatives you give oranges to today, may give you a stem of bananas next week. These generalized exchange systems assure that families have access to some of each good produced in the community.

Finally, food exchanges between relatives create safety nets to assure that all families have sufficient goods. A hunter who wounds himself with the machete, or the woman who burns herself seriously in the fire, may be unable to care for their family. Or the family who recently arrived from another tapyí may find itself without a garden. Exchanges with close kin assure that these households have at least a minimum of food.

In addition to goods, Guaraní labor is shared between households. Men seek out their male relatives to help clear their garden; women, their sisters and sisters-in-law join forces to harvest it. Work gangs sometimes include as many as eight workers. This mutual assistance not only allows people to join forces, but it relieves the tedium of what would otherwise be boring work. Women banter as they dig manioc and cut weeds. Men joke and gossip to reduce the loneliness of long treks through the forest.

This type of community exchange can be characterized as *generalized reciprocity* (Sahlins 1972:193). Exchanges are from each according to their abilities to each according to their need. The gift does not create an immediate debt for a gift of commensurate value from that person. Instead, all members are assured that when they need something, somebody in their network will provide it. The gift may not be in the form it was given, nor from the same person, but the network assures that everybody's needs are eventually satisfied.

Generalized exchanges assure that all members of the tapyí have access to the tools and resources of production. It restricts disparities of wealth and power within the community, keeping all families at a similar standard of living. Although there are no formal mechanisms that force individuals to share, there are powerful social ramifications to attempts to hoard possessions. Families who accumulate a

storehouse of food are called upon to share or suffer the criticism of their compatriots. People ridicule friends or relatives
who do not share labor saving tools. In fact, retreating from
these exchange networks calls into question a family's community membership.

Guaraní Trade

The second type of exchange in Guaraní society is with distant kin in other tapyí. In these exchanges, individuals expect
a return for the good they give. A Guaraní from another kin
group who took a fancy to Kai Taní's knife would be expected
to offer something in return. This counter gift would need to
be of roughly the same value, maybe a particularly nice baseball hat or a roll of wire.

Many people come to Itanaramí from distant Guaraní
communities in search of medical attention from Avarijú. Avarijú is an accomplished herbalist, collecting plants and pre-
paring effective medicines for many ailments, such as
diarrhea and parasites. Even in cases when he cannot provide
a clear pharmacological cure, his elixirs invariably provide
some relief. He collects his pharmacopeia in the forests surrounding Itanaramí, harvesting roots, berries, foliage and the
tender fibers underneath the bark of trees. A quick catalogue
I made of his plant knowledge showed that almost all plants
of the forest have some medicinal uses, and he has a prescrip-
tion for almost all native diseases.

Although Avarijú treats members of his own tapyí within
the framework for generalized exchange, Guaraní from other
tapyí are expected to compensate Avarijú with a gift. This
gratuity is not defined in advance nor is its value explicitly
negotiated. The giver is expected to be generous and thought-
ful. Avarijú is especially appreciative of patients who arrive
bearing gifts of toucan or macaw feathers. He uses these
feathers as religious decorations and they are worthy of the
sacred power of his medicines. Patients present their gifts to
Avarijú either before or after being treated. He is not embar-
rassed, however, to casually admire something his patient
owns and suggest how much he would like to own it. The re-
quests are not always immediately granted; many tense mo-

ments sometimes pass as patients try to negotiate the exchange without offending Avarijú.

Exchanges between distant kin and Guaraní acquaintances can be termed *balanced reciprocity*. Equal values flow between two trading partners. While in generalized reciprocity a compensatory gift is not expected from the recipient, in balanced exchanges the giver demands something in return from that specific individual. Thus, trading partners form a dyad. Rather than saying that "what goes around, comes around," here one would suggest that "what goes to you, comes back from you." This repayment need not be immediate, but both members are aware that the debt remains outstanding until the value has been returned. Neither partner intends to extract a profit from the transaction, nor wishes to lose wealth.

Guaraní Producers and Mestizo Patrons

Not all economic exchanges are among Guaraní. Indigenous people sell yerba, skins, honey and labor to mestizos in nearby Paraguayan communities. These inter-ethnic exchanges occur under a third set of social rules. Rather than generalized or balanced reciprocity, Guaraní enter trading relations with hope to give as little as possible and receive as much as they can. This type of exchange is often termed *negative reciprocity*. Both parties hope that the gift they offer in the transaction will be returned with greater value, that the trade will result in a net flow of value to them. In short, both people intend to make a profit and assume that their trading partner does as well.

Although Tangará grows most of his food, he also enjoys soap, salt and cooking oil. These goods are not available in Itanaramí, nor from his Guaraní acquaintances in other tapýi. To get access to salt, Tangará must enter the market economy and bargain with a mestizo for goods brought from the capital city. His desire for salt will most likely lead him to gather up his excess yerba and set out for one of the general stores that dot the muddy streets of the nearby frontier town.

Although the Guaraní could isolate themselves from the market economy, they choose not to. The average Guaraní family depends on local stores for basic cooking supplies, clothes and a few small luxuries. A survey of Guaraní expenditures shows that almost half of Guaraní expenditures are for food. Purchases include flour products, meat, rice, beans, lard and salt. These not only add diversity to the Guaraní diet, they give families access to basic necessities when hunting fails or between harvests. Clothing accounts for about a third of Guaraní expenses. Although most Guaraní prefer to work in simple soccer shorts or a skirt, many adults have an outfit of imported, polyester clothing for dressy occasions. The rest of Guaraní purchases go for tools, medicine or an occasional treat.

Guaraní earn cash by collecting yerba leaf from the forests surrounding their communities and selling it to local and regional patrons. In addition, Guaraní men cut fence posts, collect citrus leaves and sell animal skins for cash.

The Guaraní are suspicious of their patrons. Despite the fact that many Paraguayans have worked with the Guaraní for decades, their transactions are primarily self- interested. Patrons seek to maximize their profit by convincing Guaraní to accept the lowest possible price for the leaf. Patrons are wary of Guaraní producers as well. The Guaraní yerba gatherer seeks to take home the greatest profit possible from the yerba he brought to market. These two self-interested traders must bargain to discover a price they both are satisfied with. If no price can be arrived at, they will separate and seek new business partners elsewhere.

The traders have good reason to be suspicious of one another. Each tries to manipulate the other. Buyers have greater knowledge of the national market and try to convince the Guaraní that the price of yerba is low. They often short change sellers in the weighing or the math of the transaction. The Guaraní producer, in turn, will exaggerate the quality of the leaf or may even weight it down with sand or other leaves.

The exchange between Guaraní and mestizo takes place within the context of a hierarchical social relationship. The mestizos of the region once lived in fear of the Guaraní of the forest. Over the last century, however, the Paraguayan military and rural caudillos have established their authority in rural areas, using brutality to avenge any wrongdoing, especially any misdeeds they perceive by the Guaraní. The mestizo merchant, then, has the might of the state defending his business. The Guaraní, on the other hand, have little recourse when they are swindled in trade. This places the Guaraní trader at a disadvantage to the mestizo merchant and increases the profits of Paraguayan patrons.

The social tie between the mestizo patron and the Guaraní producer is fundamentally different from links among the Guaraní. Among the Guaraní, exchanges flow along kinship ties and are both a personal and permanent tie. Relations between Guaraní and patron are for the prime purpose of transacting business and can be dissolved by either partner. Trading among Guaraní is based on equality and trust; trading across ethnic lines is characterized by power and suspicion. Each party enters the transaction with self-interest and expects the same of the other.

In sum, Guaraní society is organized through kin relations. The ties between parent, children, and siblings provide the infrastructure for religious, political, and economic activity. Family connections determine where you reside, who you can marry, and where you can farm. This kinship network also serves as the primary arena for religious activity. Older men gather their progeny and other relatives around them, asserting kin connections to draw ever wider groups together into community and ethnic identities. Kin connections serve as political relations as well. Older leaders provide guidance and direction to their followers, calling on religious knowledge to legitimize their claim as guides for individual behavior and representatives of communal desires. Finally, kinship serves as the primary arena for economic relations. Family connections distribute goods and services throughout the community, assuring that the needs of all are attended to. Even in cases where Guaraní engage in economic exchanges with non-relatives, they do so in distinct and fundamentally different spheres.

3

Guaraní Production

The Guaraní reap a good living from the forest. The first
conquistadors in the region were impressed by the bountiful
harvests and the fat game of the Guaraní. "They want for
nothing, they have abundant fruit in their gardens and their
traps seem to attract game that keep them well fed. They
never lack for honey, corn or meat." (Cabeza de Vaca 1555/
1891) We could say the same of the Guaraní today. Although
Guaraní gardens may look unkempt to the newcomer, they
produce an abundance of corn, beans, squash and an array of
other edibles. Guaraní bring game from the forest and fish
from the streams. After four centuries, the trees of this verdant paradise are still weighed down by fruit and honey.
Contemporary Guaraní production differs from that
observed by the first conquistadors, in that Guaraní now produce for commercial markets as well. Today, in addition to
corn and meat, the Guaraní have access to salt, soap, cloth
and tools that the forest cannot produce.

TROPICAL ECOSYSTEMS

Lowland South American forests are among the most diverse
on earth. These lush, green ecosystems may have as many as
75 percent of all known plant species. Walking into the forest,
a newcomer's eye is often struck by the chaos of plant growth.
Unlike temperate forests, where one or two species dominate,

tropical flora is extremely diverse. Plants grow in a profusion of layers: the undergrowth, a lower canopy, the vines that climb and hang from branches, a second canopy, and the epiphytes that take root on the tallest branches. The variety often confuses even the trained eye of the botanist. Surveys show that while there are hundreds of species per hectare, there are usually only a few individuals of each.

The verdant growth hides the fact that the resource base on which tropical systems depend is among the most inhospitable on earth. Forest soils are under constant attack from the elements. The direct sunlight quickly breaks down nutrients in the soil and the harsh rains wash them away in torrents of muddy water that leave rivers clogged with particulate matter. The clay soils that remain lack fertility and, when exposed to the sun, quickly harden into an impenetrable layer. Forest soils anchor the forest, but do not provide water or nutrients. Thus, plants look to one another for nutrients.

Lowland forest plant species have solved their resource problems by being interdependent. Species' needs are woven together in a tightly integrated ecosystem. As plants grow and die, nutrients pass among the various layers as parasitic species feast on their rotting neighbors. Water moves between layers as well, evaporating off lower leaves, condensing in the canopy, and dripping below again. The canopy also protects the soils the forest needs to grow. Dense covers shelter the ground from harsh sunlight and deflect the strength of the torrential rains.

These tropical ecosystems are among the most fragile on earth. If one element of the system is lost, it disturbs the flow of nutrients for all other plants. Removing a single specie inhibits the growth of all those plants that depend on it. Removing a major component, such as the upper canopy, destroys the entire forest.

INDIGENOUS KNOWLEDGE

Indigenous peoples in lowland South America have developed highly organized systems to exploit the forest resources, without undermining the integrity of the tropical ecosystem. These activities are as integrated as the forests' own growth. When Avarijú leaves his house in the morning, his activities at first seem poorly organized. He may set out to work in his field, only to be distracted by an armadillo that crosses his path. Abandoning his garden work, Avarijú may spend the morning digging the animal out of its burrow. Or he may work intensely to plant his crop, then devote himself to fishing and not return to his garden for several weeks. However, these activities are not haphazard. They fit into a carefully organized system that assures that his family will always be able to satisfy its needs.

Over the thousands of years that the Guaraní have inhabited the forests, they have experimented with a variety of ways to earn a living from it. With their intimate knowledge of the diversity of plants, and their close attention to the soils and the water systems, indigenous people have adapted their production patterns to fit the highly evolved ecosystem of the lowland forests. Far from being primitive or uncivilized, indigenous peoples have a highly developed production system.

Guaraní Agroforestry

Indigenous agroforestry does not replace the existing ecosystem, but builds on it, mimicking both the structure and the process of the tropical forest. First, indigenous production systems are diverse, like the organization of forest. This diversity allows forest residents to exploit a variety of ecological niches. Secondly, indigenous production systems depend on the resources of plants and animals, rather than on the scarce nutrients of tropical soils. Fertility is cycled from nature to human use and returned to the larger ecosystem, bringing agroforestry into dynamic equilibrium with nature. Throughout Latin America, farmers have learned that by diversifying their production activities, they avoid over-exploiting any specific resource. Like the forest system itself, indigenous people spread out their dependence on a series of resources. By moderate use of the soils, the water, the canopy, and the fauna, forest residents assure that the entire ecosystem will continue to function.

As discussed in the first chapter, agroforestry integrates tree crops with agriculture, domestic animal raising, and other activities. Some agroforestry systems are closely managed by the farmer. In Costa Rica, for example, banana trees are planted over coffee trees, and cattle graze on pasture underneath the canopy (Clay 1989). In contrast, the agroforestry of most indigenous groups are much less structured. In systems such as Guaraní agroforestry, the forest canopy is often left intact and existing area plants managed and harvested for human use.

Guaraní agroforestry is composed of three general types of activities: horticulture, hunting and fishing, and gathering. These three activities integrate to assure that Guaraní have sufficient food throughout the year. Diversity reduces the economic disruption created by seasonal changes in garden production, declining hunting populations, crop pests, or the market. Although Avarijú's daily tasks may seem poorly organized to the newcomer, he is shifting between different productive sectors to use his time and resources efficiently.

The different sectors of the Guaraní economy demand two primary resources: human labor and physical resources. Integrating various production activities demands that these resources be carefully allocated. The Guaraní do not allow their use of one physical resource to conflict with the protection of another. For example, they do not cut down the high canopy that protects the thin, tropical soils. Labor resources need to be protected as well. Since each family must provide labor for all the various production spheres, Guaraní carefully arrange their work to assure that workers are free when needed in each activity.

Gardening

If one were to ask Avarijú what his primary work was, he would say gardening. With a little prodding, he would take you on a tour of his garden. He would lead you down the small path that enters the forest behind his house, over the small stream, and up the opposite bank to an opening in the forest. With his machete, he would point with pride to the size of the half acre clearing, about as big as a city house lot, and call your attention to the towering corn stalks and bursting bean pod.

Corn, beans and manioc are most important in the Guaraní garden, supplemented by peanut, banana, sweet potato, and sugar cane. Although most crops are seasonal, planted once or at most twice a year, Guaraní plant manioc sufficient to provide a constant supply of the tuber throughout the year. Manioc provides a basic starch for Guaraní families, but it is low in nutrition and needs to be supplemented by other foods.

Rather than isolating crops into different plots, Guaraní farmers plant the full diversity of their crops in a single plot. It is not uncommon for a gardener to have ten or twelve different crops interplanted in one garden. Moreover, Guaraní plant several varieties of each crop. Thus, there may be six or seven types of corn and the same number of kinds of sweet potato, manioc, beans and bananas.

The new visitor would probably be struck by the chaotic profusion of the garden's growth. Bean vines climb corn stalks, sweet potato winds its way around the stems of the manioc, and banana plants erupt unexpectedly throughout the plot. The growth is not confused. Avarijú carefully arranges his field to maximize production. Each crop is interplanted with another that helps it grow. He plants corn and beans in the same hole so that the fast-growing corn stalks can provide poles for the climbing bean vines. Manioc leaves provide the shade needed by the more delicate sweet potato plants. This diversity creates a microcosm of the larger forest. In structure, the canopy of banana and manioc shelters the soils, and a profusion of sweet potato and squash vines climb through the growth. In process, plants are grown in the debris of the forest, and the refuse from one harvest becomes fertilizer for the next crop.

Guaraní gardening is often called *horticulture* or *shifting agriculture*. It differs from more conventional agriculture in that crops are rarely planted in the same soil for more than three years, as new plots are periodically cut into the forest. Gardening follows the wet and dry seasons, with the annual cycle generally opposite that of the northern hemisphere. Avarijú usually begins to clear his garden in July. With machete in hand, he scans the forest and soils for a suitable spot. The topsoils under high forests usually have the greatest fertility. The experienced farmer will usually choose an area where the deeper soil is reddish, signaling a good mixture of sand and clay. Guaraní gardeners avoid higher sandy areas, where soils are hot and dry, in favor of the gradual slopes along small streams. This assures that roots will have water, yet protects them from the saturation of floodplain soils.

When a suitable location has been chosen, Guaraní men clear the forest with machetes and axes. The small trees are chopped down, bringing much of the canopy and vines (*liana*) crashing to earth in a tangled mass. Larger trees are left standing, but the bark near the base is stripped off, killing the tree. Without foliage, the dry trunks do not hinder the garden and are blown over after several years. The work is hot and heavy. It is common for fathers, sons, brothers and cousins to join forces, clearing each person's plot in turn. This not only speeds the work, but provides companionship in the lonely forest.

Farmers clear land in the dry season, from July through September, before the start of the October rains. At this time of year it only takes a couple of weeks for the sun to dry the forest detritus. Procrastinators pay a high price. Once spring showers begin, the forest reclaims its land even before the confusion of brush, vines and tree trunks turns brown.

When the forest debris is as dry as tinder, the Guaraní build small fires in the underbrush and it erupts in an inferno. The cool, damp forest stops the raging fire at the edge of the plot. If one burning does not complete the task, and it rarely does, the family returns the next day to pile the remaining branches and relight the fire.

This slash and burn technique is an extremely efficient use of the overstory. The fire releases nutrient compounds that are otherwise bound in wood and foliage and leaves a coat of fertile ash over the soil. By using nutrients from the forest cover to fertilize their crops, the Guaraní mimic the forest's own process of recycling nutrients among plant populations in a closed system. In this case, nutrients are shifted from forest plants to cultivated crops.

When the spring rains arrive, entire families go to the fields to plant crops. A hole is poked in the soft earth with a simple, sharpened pole. A couple of seeds, or a bud from a manioc stalk is dropped into each. Finally, the planters kick dirt into the hole and tamp the spot with their heel. Guaraní place plants approximately a meter apart, but may plant three or four different crops over the same ground. Consequently, there are often four or five different plants in each square meter.

After the garden is planted, field work is finished for several weeks. Abundant spring rains water the crops during the critical growing season. Tender shoots erupt from the fresh soils. As crops mature, there are few pests or competitors to hinder their growth. Grasses and plants of the forest cannot withstand the direct sun and rain of the garden, allowing crops to grow without competition. The insects of the dark, damp forest, also find the dry air of the garden intolerable and ignore the growing crops. Consequently, families often travel after planting their crops, returning weeks later to find the crops ready to harvest.

The arrival of the first crops is cause for celebration in Itanaramí. The ripening of the first corn in February signals the end of the annual food shortages and ushers in a period of abundance. Families who have been without corn and beans for months, have more than they can eat. The end of the *karuvaí*, the hunger season, is the time for religious gatherings and initiation rites. Besides initiating new members, the mita-mongaraií ceremoniously welcomes the garden crops. Corn is of central significance to Guaraní society, a fact that is clear in these ceremonies. Corn stalks are gathered and laid against the wooden vat of fermented corn and, as the religious leader divines the names of the new children, he recognizes the corn and initiates it into the community.

It is men's task to clear the plot, but harvesting is women's work. Women leave the house each morning with children in tow to dig manioc, pick beans and harvest corn. By February, corn and beans are ready to be collected. As the season progresses, the peanuts, rice, and squash mature. Like men, women join forces to work in their gardens. The otherwise tedious task is relieved with joking and singing. By mid-morning, they have returned with bags of corn or manioc balanced on their heads, ready to cook for the midday meal.

The annual garden cycle ends in August as garden plots are depleted. This begins the start of karuvaí. Even when harvests are abundant, it is difficult to store foods for the coming cold months. Birds, peccary and deer eat whatever remains in the field, and insects attack the stores in houses. Thus, by September, most gardens are reduced to manioc and sweet potato and families are forced to look elsewhere for food.

The annual cycle of gardening builds into a longer cycle of garden shifting. Despite the gardens' ability to mimic the forest, clearing exposes the soils to the rigors of the intense sun, rains and competition from insect and plant pests. Warmth from the sun breaks up compounds and harsh rains wash them out of the soils. Corn and beans demand considerable nitrogen from the thin soils. Fertility soon declines. Moreover, as time passes, pests and weeds find their way into the plot. Grasshoppers and grubs discover the clearing and reproduce quickly on the vulnerable crops. Grasses, when they finally are introduced, quickly colonize and cover the exposed soils. When gardeners replant beans in the same area for a second or third year, they find that vines are stunted and seeds are littered with weevils.

Rather than simply abandoning gardens after a single productive season, Guaraní plant them with crops that can thrive on poorer soils. Manioc and sweet potato demand little of the soils and are resistant to the weeds and insects that invade corn and beans. As women uproot manioc and sweet potato each morning, they replant buds in the holes. The buds grow through the tangled chaos of old fields with almost no maintenance. Although tubers take nine months to mature, these crops produce continuously for up to four years. This assures a constant supply of basic food with very little work.

After the fourth and fifth years, when even manioc fails to prosper, the Guaraní plant banana and other tree crops. These are not hindered by the weeds and brush that overtake the plot. In fact, the plot produces many edible plants after the forest canopy reclaims the sky over the garden.

Guaraní gardeners exploit several areas at the same time. Farmers continue to work old plots even as new plots are cut. The annual cycle of clearing, planting and abandonment builds into a multiyear cycle, where farmers exploit parcels of a variety of ages, using each for a different type of production. These plots often abut. Where one end of a gardener's plot may be freshly cut, the other side may be an aging banana plot that is being reclaimed by the forest.

When gardens are no longer cultivated, the forest quickly takes over the plot. The forest colonizes the plot from the edge toward the center. Vines send tendrils into the sunlight and roots of the trees at the plot's edge burst through the soil with saplings. Bats and birds feeding on the insects in the garden drop seeds into the weeds, as do foraging deer, peccary and armadillos. Within a decade of clearing it is difficult to identify a plot; within twenty years the high canopy has been replaced and the forest ecosystem has restructured itself. Weeds and insects that prosper in the broken earth and the intense sunlight are driven off. Species that flourish in the moist shade of the forest replace them.

The shifting of gardens and houses builds into larger community movements. As gardeners seek out fertile soils for farming, they eventually destroy the high forest near their houses. As Avarijú destroys the high forest near his house, he and his family are forced to walk farther and farther to bring in crops. Guaraní houses are rudimentary wooden frames with simple roofs that can easily be built with a few days' labor. After a point, it is easier to move their house than trek over muddy paths with heavy loads. Families will then dissemble their houses and haul the beams and thatch to the edge of their new garden.

Every several decades, Guaraní move their communities to new areas of the forest. The death of a religious leader often spurs this shift. His body is placed on a bier inside the house and the houses of his followers are abandoned. The community builds new houses at another site in the high forest. It is useful to note that the pattern of the religious exoduses coincides with the ecological cycle. After several decades of population increase and garden clearing, it is not uncommon for a community to be surrounded by infertile, dry fallow. Relocating at the death of a religious leader, which happens every two or three decades, moves Guaraní families when they are also being forced to walk several kilometers to find fertile garden land.

Hunting, Fishing, and Gathering

In addition to gardening, Guaraní harvest materials from the standing forest to satisfy their subsistence needs. When Avarijú abandons his garden to chase an armadillo or spend a day fishing, he forages, rather than produces his family needs. The Guaraní depend on the forest for food during the months when the garden is bare. Fishing, trapping, and gathering provide critical protein when corn and beans are gone. As the harvest drags on and manioc and sweet potato become scarcer, wild tubers and forest honey provide important carbohydrates to supplement their diet.

Hunting is a primary means for the Guaraní to get protein in the forest. Although the stereotype is of an indigenous hunter with bow or lance, Guaraní prefer to trap animals. Walking down a community path, it is not uncommon to see a deadfall balanced over a game trail or a snare for deer or peccary at the edge of a garden. Gardens are favorite places to trap animals. Deer and paca are attracted to the tender crops, armadillo and peccary dig manioc and sweet potatoes. In fact, Guaraní make little effort to restrict forest animals from their gardens, preferring to set traps around the perimeter and harvest game as it tries to enter.

Traps are built with local materials. Hunters often simply suspend large palm trunks over corn or fruit bait and fix a trigger underneath. These deadfalls are especially useful for small animals, such as paca, armadillo, monkeys, and birds. This basic idea is sometimes elaborated into complex contraptions that defy the eye's ability to untangle the interconnections. In monkey traps the falling log closes the door to a small woven chamber, securing the animal without hurting it. To catch birds in gardens, the trigger drops a woven basket over the corn bait.

The Guaraní also are skilled snare builders. They spin the fiber of the Caraguatá plant into strong twine, which camouflages easily on the forest floor. Hunters suspend a twine noose from a bent sapling, which tightens when the animal disturbs it. Guaraní snares lift the head or a leg of the animal. By taking the creature's weight off the ground it makes it difficult for it to struggle loose. Snares are used to kill heavy game. A simple noose on a trail can hold a deer or peccary. When positioned over a covered pit it can hold a tapir (*Tapirus terrestris*). Some Guaraní have even use baited snares to catch large cats, such as the jaguar (*Panthera onca*).

Although they prefer to trap game, Guaraní sometimes hunt with arms. Bows were often used in the past, but today only old or poor men cut bows and fashion arrows. In most communities, at least one family has purchased an old shotgun, and most men can borrow one for a night's hunting. In exchange, hunters are usually generous in sharing their meat with the gun's owner.

Rather than stroll through the forest in the day, the preferred method of sport hunters, Guaraní hunt from trees at night. They often build a stand over a game trail or in their garden, then wait motionlessly for their quarry. This is extremely effective, but excruciatingly boring and terribly uncomfortable. Only the most committed hunter can withstand hours of incessant assault by the mosquitoes that fill the night air.

Fishing is another source of dependable protein that can be harvested in the forest. Rivers flood their low banks during the rainy season, inundating a broad plain on both sides. Oxbow lakes left behind by a meandering river are filled by the flooding. Fish are trapped in the lagoons as the rivers subside at the end of the wet season.

Poisons are a favorite way for Guaraní to kill many fish quickly. The bark of the timbo plant is crushed and washed through the water, leaving a thin seal over the surface of the lagoon. Once the water is poisoned, the fishermen sit around, sometimes for hours, waiting for the poison to take effect. They relax at the lagoon's edge, gossiping or sleeping until the water is depleted of oxygen. The stunned fish rise to the surface and can be collected by hand. While poison is extremely effective, it ruins the lagoon for future fishing, and usually provides more fish than families can eat. Therefore,

Guaraní use poison on smaller or more distant lagoons, using lines or nets in larger lagoons near communities.

Many men prefer to fish with hook and nylon line. This method is quicker than poison and allows fishermen to target a specific variety of fish they prefer. Guaraní fish lagoons at night, because the fish are most active after dark. Fishermen leave their houses in the late afternoon. For bait, they collect wasp larva and use them to catch minnows. Arriving at the lagoon at dusk, they build a roaring fire against the night and settle down to fish. Nylon line is tied to a sapling and a minnow is baited on the hook. Fishermen then toss the bait into the murky water and slap the surface of the lagoon with the end of the pole to attract the fish's attention.

Guaraní are reluctant to spend the night in the forest; there are too many dangers - animals, humans, and especially the supernatural. So men fish with relatives and friends whose gossip and stories make the long hours pass more quickly. A favorite pastime of the men of Itanaramí was to convince a reluctant anthropologist to join them in the mosquito filled night. He provided hours of mirth as he swatted bugs and vainly tried to catch something to eat. When fishing is good, the night is punctuated by yells and laughter as fish are pulled unceremoniously onto the bank. Guaraní prefer small catfish (e.g. *Pimelodus charias*) for their size and taste, although they will eat almost any fish they catch, including mud eels (*Symbranchus marmoratus*).

The fishing season starts in December, as the lowlands dry enough to allow travel on the floodplains. It ends as the lagoons are fished out in late February. Consequently, fishing returns are the greatest in these months between planting and harvest, when Guaraní are most in need of food. It is harder to catch the large river fish, but the *surubí* (*Pimelodus tigrinus*) and *dorado* (*Salmonidae*) grow to twenty kilograms. These are divvied up by the community or sold for cash to mestizos. Catching a lunker catfish is a windfall for the community, but not a predictable source of food for a family.

Guaraní collect a variety of other subsistence goods from the forest. During the dry season in April, May and June, families make excursions to orange groves in the forests or berry patches in the marshy grasslands. Honey is also a favorite reason for a day trip. There are nine varieties of forest bees, and several produce succulent honey. People watch these bees carefully, tracing their flight to the nest, and harvesting the honey.

A family traveling through the forest can usually find a meal easily. The hearts can be cut out of palm trees as a nutritious salad; fruit collected from a myriad of trees; or filling roots dug from forest plants. Hungry travelers can even get a good meal from insects. The larva of bamboo moths and the abdomen of leaf cutter ants are not only tasty, but extremely high in fat.

In addition to food, the Guaraní can satisfy almost all their other needs from the forest. Building materials, for example, are readily available. Tall marsh grasses are cut for thatch and the roof timbers are cut from the abundant hardwood. Guaraní also make forest medicines. Tropical plants have high concentrations of powerful organic substances, called alkaloids. Guaraní specialists concentrate these alkaloids to manufacture effective medicines for many sicknesses. Even salt can be collected from forest lowlands and purified into a satisfying condiment.

Commercial Harvesting

Guaraní collect a variety of forest goods to sell into regional markets. Yerba mate, animal skins, essential oils, and food are all harvested from the forest. These provide cash and manufactured commodities from national and international markets. In terms of production, commercial collecting differs little from indigenous subsistence activities. As in their gardening, Guaraní are careful to harvest forest materials without degrading the ecological integrity of the larger system. First, commercial collecting uses the forest extensively, but not intensively. For example, collectors cut foliage from all yerba trees, but harvest only the mature leaves of each tree every third year. This protects the plants' survival.

Second, as subsistence production exploits a variety of ecological niches (e.g. soil, flora, and fauna) the Guaraní harvest a variety of goods for sale. Consequently, families do not over-exploit a commodity in a desperate attempt to earn cash.

As families need more money, or as the market for a commodity declines, they harvest and market a different resource. By collecting different goods for sale, families generate income throughout the year. When the yerba harvest is finished in May, the Guaraní shift their energy to hunting skins for cash. When fur quality declines in September, they cut fence posts. Consequently, families follow an annual cycle, harvesting for a variety of commercial markets over the year.

The most important source of income for the Guaraní is the sale of yerba leaves into the national and international markets. *Ilex paraguayensis* is closely related to the holly tree and grows to about thirty-five feet. It prefers low soils and shade, thriving under the broken canopy along streams and the edges of marshes. The Guaraní call these areas *ka'atí*, which derives from the Guaraní word *ka'á*, which means yerba. Although it is common throughout the region, yerba does not grow in dense stands and rarely comprises more than 10 percent of the forest cover.

Yerba is gathered at the end of the annual growing season, when the leaves are thick and full of alkaloids. Men, alone or in pairs, set up temporary camp in a dense growth of yerba. Yerba leaves grow on the thinnest twigs, which protrude from all areas of the thick trunk and branches like the suckers of an apple tree. Each half-meter branch has between eight and a dozen leaves. Working with sharp, short machetes, they climb into trees, clip twigs and drop the foliage to the ground.

Guaraní commercial cutting takes care not to damage yerba trees. Yerba gatherers, called *mineros* know not to harvest any branches thicker than their little thumb. This limits cutting to twigs that have foliage and protects the branches on which they grow. In addition, Guaraní harvesters harvest each tree every three years. This assures that plants are allowed to recover their size and health after each harvest. The collector who ignores these rules earns a bad name among his compatriots. These simple practices guarantee that the harvest will not reduce the productive capacity or the reproductive ability of the tree.

The first step in drying yerba is to scorch the leaves, a process called *ohapy*. Collectors wave small bundles of boughs through the flames of an intense fire. This converts water in the foliage to steam, bursting the thin membrane on the underside of each leaf with a sound like popping corn. This prevents the leaves from rotting quickly and lets them dry slowly.

After scorching, the minero ties the twigs into heavy bundles and carries them to his forest camp. There, he piles the leaves on a large drying rack called a *mbarbakuá*. Mbarbakuá are constructed from stakes and poles. Saplings are stuck in the ground about a half-meter apart to form an oval three meters long. The yerbatero then doubles the tops over and ties them to one another, forming a loose dome-shaped platform for the yerba. A second set of poles are then placed in the ground, but angled outward. Their tips are attached with a circle of thin branches to form a railing to keep the foliage on the platform. Finally, the yerbatero digs a fire pit beside the platform and hollows a cavity underneath the mbarbakuá, with an opening to allow smoke and heat to filter up through the leaves.

Drying racks can hold up to sixty kilos of fresh yerba leaf, about as much as a man can collect in a day's work. The scorched leaves are placed loosely on the frame and a fire is lit in the pit underneath. For twenty-four hours, yerbateros feed the fire and turn the leaf with long handled rakes, allowing it to dry evenly and slowly. Men prefer to work in teams. Not only do they share the labor of collecting firewood and feeding the flame, but companionship alleviates the boredom.

When the foliage has been thoroughly dried, Guaraní open the side of the mbarbakuá and spill the yerba onto the ground. The leaf is crushed and chopped with poles and machetes. Finally, the minero packs the course tea into burlap sacks for shipment to market.

A second important source of cash for Guaraní is citrus oil, called *esencia*. Essential oils are extracted from the leaves of bitter orange trees (*Vulgaris vulgaris*), which grow in stands in the forest. This essence of orange is used in perfume and as a natural flavor for food. The collection of orange leaves is similar to that of yerba. When the foliage has reached its fullest, men climb into the trees and trim off the twigs that hold the most leaves. Like yerba collection, the production of esencia involves harvesting only the foliage of the citrus plants, most of which grows on shoots off the main branches.

Rather than dry leaves, collectors distill the heavy oils from the foliage in rudimentary stills that they build in the forest. A location is chosen near both firewood and a stream. Oil drums, copper tubing and wooden troughs are fashioned together with wire and rope. Water and leaves are packed into the metal drum and, when fired up, it sputters, smokes, and belches. Eventually, a thin stream of pungent, heavy oil is siphoned off the steaming brew through a shallow trough into a metal tin.

The sale of animal skins is a third source of cash for the Guaraní. The national and international footwear market demands a variety of leathers. Although the Guaraní hunt primarily for meat, much of the game they kill has valuable hides and skins. Two of the favorite quarry, deer (*Mazama americanus*) and peccary, have skins that are easy to sell on the domestic leather market. People kill lizards (*Tupinambis teguixin*), caiman, and snakes, but flesh of these animals is less desirable and their skins harder to sell. Some animals are killed solely for their pelts. Few Guaraní will eat the meat of the South American fox (*Dusicyon gymnocercus*), but will hunt it for its pelt. Until 1979, the Guaraní set snares for jaguar and ocelot and sold the skins at high prices into the international market. This trade was stopped by international restrictions on the sale of furs from endangered species. Today, few Guaraní take the time or the risks to kill forest cats.

A final method of earning cash from the forest is the sale of timber products. Guaraní often fell and market selected hardwood into the international market. The extremely dense Urundeymí (*Astronium urundeuva*), for example, is often sold as fenceposts. This wood can withstand years of exposure to water; some timbers cut for the 18th century missions still stand strong and firm in the ruins of the Jesuit churches. This resistance to decay makes the wood ideal for fences in eastern Paraguay's moist soils. Urundeymí grows throughout the canopied forests of the Mbaracayú area, but at very low densities. Men have to search out mature trees, cut a trail to their bases, and fell the timbers with axes within the close confines of the forest. While the technology is simple and cheap, the labor is heavy, slow, and unpleasant. Mosquitoes and sweat bees quickly fill the moist, still air of the forest and cover the bodies of the men. Once down, the timber is cut into two meter sections and split into rails. The loggers use wooden mauls to drive iron wedges into small cracks, forcing the dense wood to give way along its straight grain. Eventually, the trunk is divided into fence poles of approximately ten centimeters in diameter. Men carry these on their backs to a dirt track, where oxen take the load to a dirt road. Logging trucks carry the poles to market, either into Brazil or south to Paraguay's ranching area.

In sum, Guaraní horticulture, hunting, fishing, and commercial gathering integrate into a single agroforestry system. Guaraní agroforestry provides families with a variety of sources for food. This assures them a diverse diet and helps reduce the seasonal shortages in any one sector. Moreover, agroforestry gives households access to cash as well as subsistence goods. Commercial collecting provides families access to market products, without pulling them away from their gardens and traps.

AGROFORESTRY AS ADAPTION

Guaraní agroforestry is adapted to the tropical ecosystem. Two aspects of the system protect the forest, even as it provides a satisfactory life for the Guaraní. First, agroforestry exploits diverse ecological niches, assuring that no single resource will be over-harvested. Second, Guaraní production uses small areas of the forest for a short time, then moves on and allows the ecosystem to regenerate. By exploiting the forest extensively, in both time and space, the Guaraní avoid the damage caused by intensive long-term exploitation of small areas.

Production Diversity

Guaraní agroforestry exploits a variety of niches in the tropical ecosystem. Horticulture makes use of the dense flora, converting the overstory and underbrush to fertilizer for the thin forest soils. Burning the plant material frees the carbon, potassium and other nutrients critical to plant growth. Conventional agriculture depends on thick loam soils with high fertility and replaces nutrients with concentrated fertilizers refined from petroleum. There are no fertile soils and few fertilizers in the forest. Consequently, horticulture uses the infertile soils simply to hold plants, depending on the flora of the forest to fertilize their growth.

Unlike conventional agriculture, horticulture exploits the variety of nutrients within thin tropical soils. As we have seen, Guaraní interplant many different plant crops in a plot. Diversity reduces the number of plants of any one crop in the garden and increases the crop varieties in an area. As crops differ in nutritional needs, this interplanting maximizes the use of diverse, but scarce, resources in the soil. This diversity in gardens mimics the natural environment. Tropical forests, themselves, are extremely diverse, allowing plants to maintain stable communities on scarce soil resources.

Hunting and fishing exploit a second set of resource niches in the tropical ecosystem. Traps harvest animals that forage in the warm, moist shade of the forest canopy. Deer, tapir, peccary, paca and armadillo convert the forest's plant material into protein that can be processed by humans. When hunting fails, men collect fish, caimans and turtles that feed in the slow moving rivers and ox-bow lakes. Fishing captures the rivers' fertility for human use. Fishing is especially important in resource diversification, in that moving waters bring fish that replenish streams and flood-plain lakes near indigenous communities. When tasty game or fish are unavailable, Guaraní shift their hunting skills to less desirable foods. If needed, Guaraní will kill monkeys and anteaters, gather ants and grubs, or fish for minnows and eels. Each will provide a filling and nutritious meal, even if it is less appetizing.

By exploiting a variety of animals, the Guaraní avoid over-exploiting any one population. Guaraní prefer to harvest animals near their communities, rather than travel longer distances to hunt one favorite type of game, such as deer. Even the guinea pigs (*Cavia aperea*) that live in the grasses around their houses can provide a good meal. Families will eat just about any bird or animal if other meat becomes scarce. This increases the hunting pressure on all game populations in a small area, but reduces the demands on any one population.

The nutrition won from the fauna and insects of the forest reduces the Guaraní need to produce great quantities of high-protein food in their gardens. This reduces the size of their gardens and preserves a larger portion of the region in a forested state. Conversely, with some protein in their garden, Guaraní are not forced to exterminate the last of any one game population as it becomes scarce. By dividing their food demands between two niches, they protect both from being ravaged to fill short-term food shortages.

Even the commercial activities of the Guaraní are diversified over a range of ecological niches. Yerba gathering and essence production exploit the foliage of trees along the stream banks; hunting uses the furs of inedible animals; and lumbering harvests hardwood from high forests. As in food getting, this commercial diversity protects any one resource from over-exploitation. As yerba or fox become scarce near communities, Guaraní shift their commercial gathering to more readily accessible commodities, such as reptiles or citrus leaves.

Production Cycles

In addition to diversifying resource exploitation over many ecological niches, Guaraní production spreads its demands for resources over time. Annual production cycles integrate into longer sequences in which families move their gardens and communities through the forest.

The work year of a Guaraní family can be divided into four periods, each characterized by a distinct type of work. As women harvest in the gardens throughout the year and work little in wage labor or hunting, these four periods are most evident in men's work strategies. In the first work period, from July through September, households clear and plant gardens. From October through January, the second period, men spend a greater amount of time working for cash to buy food during the karuvaí. Fishing characterizes the third work period of the year, from February and March. Finally, from April through June, men divide their labor equally between forest subsistence and commercial gathering.

While gardening destroys trees and hunting reduces local game populations, these effects are on micro-environments. The amount of forest under intense exploitation at any time is less than 5 percent of the area and when these areas become inhospitable, households and communities move into new fertile areas. Over the course of a Guaraní's life, he or she might live in ten or twelve different areas, leaving behind a string of recovering micro-environments.

As the fertility returns to abandoned village sites, Guaraní return to them. The forest is vast, but there is never an abundance of ideal sites, with fertile land for farming, rivers for fishing and streams for water and washing. Guaraní return to these spots as soon as they have recovered from previous inhabitants. Thus, we can define a cycle of village movement where, over many generations, Guaraní return to places occupied by their ancestors.

The Guaraní have sustained a complex and dependable production system in the lowland forests, despite the region's fragile and scarce resources. What aspects of this economy assure its sustainability? First, the resource demands are diverse. By exploiting a variety of ecological niches in each area, the Guaraní can earn what they need without undermining the integrity of that system. Second, the resource demands of indigenous production are extensive. By spreading their horticulture, foraging and commercial gathering over a large area of the forest, they limit the intensity of transformation in any one area.

The sustainable system of the Guaraní is not simply for their subsistence; it has maintained a cash income for the Guaraní for over four centuries. The Guaraní have sold yerba from their forests since 1500 and have become dependent on the manufactured goods that it provides them. Guaraní commercial gathering abides by the same environmentally friendly strictures that govern sectors of their economy. First, the Guaraní are not dependent on a single resource for commercial wealth; they sell a variety of commodities, depending on availability and the market prices. If yerba becomes scarce or its price falls, they shift their efforts to harvesting another type of good. Second, commercial gathering is extensive, rather than intensive. Gatherers harvest specific elements of the complex ecosystem, protecting the viability of the larger structure. As demand for a product increases, new areas are exploited without increasing ecological destruction near Guaraní villages.

GENDER AND THE DIVISION OF LABOR

When early morning visitors walk into Avarijú's houselot, they generally find the entire family sitting beside the fire drinking mate. Before the dew dries off the grass, however, they will be up and working. The house needs to be swept, the blankets thrown over the rafters, and traps must be checked. As the sun warms the earth, Avarijú leaves for his trapline and his wife slides the baby onto her hip and heads for the garden. The older daughters take the dirty clothes to wash at the river and Avarijú's son grabs a machete and heads into the forest to cut yerba.

How do Guaraní spend their time? Who does what tasks? In industrial societies, workers specialize and perform only one type of work. Mechanics, steam fitters, lawyers, and daycare workers each perform a small part in a large and complex labor system. In contrast, an analysis of Guaraní labor shows that all individuals are called upon to perform a wide variety of tasks. The principal division of Guaraní labor is along gender lines. Besides horticulture, hunting, trapping, and commercial gathering, family members must maintain a building, cook food, care for children, attend to personal hygiene, as well as going to religious gatherings and community meetings.

Work time can be categorized as *productive* labor or *reproductive* labor (Minge Klevana 1980: 279). Productive labor generates the food and materials that the family needs to survive. Among the Guaraní, productive labor is the horticulture, hunting, fishing and commercial work; it is done in the forest or fields. Reproductive labor is the work necessary to see that the family group is maintained and replaced. Among the Guaraní, this work is usually done at home and consists primarily of childcare, cooking, house construction and maintenance. Where productive labor fills the household's needs on a daily basis, reproductive labor assures its continuation over generations.

Guaraní households spend an average of 18 percent of their time in productive activities. Almost a third of family labor is in horticulture, slightly less to forest subsistence strategies and about 40 percent of its production is in commercial activities. Twenty-seven percent of Guaraní household labor time is allocated to reproduction. Family members cook, care for children, organize the house, clean the yard, and sew.

Not all Guaraní time is devoted to the necessities of life. Although the Guaraní spend just about half (45.6 percent) their time working, over a third of their daylight hours are spent resting, relaxing and socializing. Work stops at nightfall, and the family again gathers around the fire to talk, think, and sleep. It is worth noting that the amount of time that the Guaraní spend resting is greater than that allowed by work schedules in more industrialized societies (Schor 1991). Guaraní men spend an average of a quarter of daylight hours working outside the home, roughly half the time needed to subsist in a European country (Minge-Klevana 1980). Far from being a group struggling to make a living in a harsh environment, the Guaraní are relatively affluent. They satisfy their needs fairly easily, using the remaining time and energy to be with family and friends.

Guaraní labor is highly organized, with each individual carrying out specific tasks as well as engaging in group-oriented work. For the most part, work is organized along gender lines. This is particularly evident in gardening, which demands the greatest total amount of labor of the three primary production activities -- an hour a day on average. Both men and women both in the garden, but they perform different tasks.

The different responsibilities lead to different work rhythms. Men's greatest work is early in the agricultural cycle as the spring rains approach. Teams of men and boys leave early for the designated garden plots and work diligently felling trees and clearing undergrowth to get a plot ready for planting. After the plot is cleared, however, males spend weeks at a time without entering the garden, devoting themselves to hunting, fishing and commercial gathering. Women, in contrast, need to harvest food from the garden every day. Most women go to the garden each morning to dig manioc and sweet potato for the daily meals. During the harvest, they may spend the entire morning there, picking beans and corn.

The Guaraní household is equally dependent on the labor of men and women. In total, women work more in the gardens, but men do most of the other productive tasks. When women head off to dig manioc or sweet potato, men go into the forest. They hunt, fish, collect produce to sell, or do paid field work. In terms of food, women bring in the garden produce, often the carbohydrates that sustain the family. Men, on the other hand, are responsible for the meat and purchased goods that the family needs.

Where men do a range of productive labor, women perform a greater portion of the reproductive tasks of the household. The responsibilities of cooking, cleaning, and childcare fall largely on the shoulders of women. The average women spends about an hour cooking each day. When a woman returns from the garden in the morning, she must peel the manioc, get water, and put the pot on to boil. Throughout the day, she is often tending a pot of rice, corn or beans. In addition, women spend three hours doing other household tasks, such as sewing and cleaning. The houselot needs to be swept and clothes washed. Childcare takes place in the midst of other work. Infants watch from a shoulder sling and toddle behind their working mother as they grow.

The economy of a Guaraní household demands the work of both men and women. The various demands of the garden, forest work, and childcare force men and women to coordinate their activities. The necessity of both sexes is clear when a man or women is forced to live alone. The recent widow, or the man whose wife has left him, is left with half a household. A man might have a new shirt or a kilo of meat, but no manioc in his garden. A single woman may have a garden teeming with produce, but no yerba to drink. Few people keep house alone. Most individuals are forced to link up with a partner or move in with relatives.

Anthropologists suggest that a person's economic contributions give them power in society. In societies where women are excluded from production, they are dependent on men for their day-to-day needs. Because of this dependence, their power is diminished in relations with men (Leacock 1972; Friedl 1978). The division of labor in Guaraní production provides women considerable independence. Women's garden work brings in a major source of food and contributes to her status within the household and community.

PRODUCTION AND GUARANÍ AUTONOMY

Besides stability and sustainability, the economy of the Guaraní has allowed them to maintain a level of autonomy from the national society. The first Europeans came into this area in the 16th century. Their mestizo descendants have had continual and, at times, intense relations with the Guaraní. The yerba market has integrated the Guaraní into an extensive international commodity market.

Despite their close contact with the larger society and economy, the Guaraní have not assimilated into it. Even as their goods flowed across cultural boundaries to Paraguayans and Brazilians, the Guaraní maintained their own identity and culture. When Avarijú sells yerba in the local mestizo town, he is very aware of the cultural distance between himself and the mestizo merchant. He lives in a different community, practices a different religion, and pays respect to a different type of political leader.

Economic independence has given the Guaraní power to maintain their cultural identity. Even as they trade in the international economy, Guaraní control the level of their involvement in it. When the prices offered for their produce drop too low, they stop selling; when merchants raise the prices on store goods, they don't buy.

Prices of yerba, skins and wood change drastically and often. Price fluctuations are often in response to international demand. Alternately, they reflect local factors, such as road conditions or transport price. The cost of goods that Guaraní buy often spirals as they become scarce. It is not uncommon for commodity prices to be doubled or halved over a single season, even without the occasional greedy merchant who wants to gouge the purchaser. These economic vagaries make it difficult to plan household budgets; Avarijú heads into the forest to collect yerba without any guarantee of the price he will be paid, nor the quantity of store goods he will be able to buy.

Fortunately, by maintaining a dependable source of subsistence from horticulture, fishing, collecting and hunting, the Guaraní do not have to rely on commercial markets. The economic stability of a Guaraní family is in their garden, not in the yerbales or the *obrajes*. The young man who professes love but does not clear a garden, is considered a Don Juan rather than a suitor. The surest sign that a young couple is going to settle down as a family is the field they plant together. It is considered risky to let a garden go fallow and depend on wage labor for food. Families who choose this route make themselves vulnerable to the whim of the market and the patron.

Many patrons have tried to use debt bondage to keep collectors working in the forests. Patrons use cash advances to draw mestizos into forest work, loans that they must work off by collecting yerba or felling timbers. Totally dependent on patrons for food and equipment, these workers are underpaid for their production and overcharged for their necessities. They become wage-slaves to the commercial economy. Guaraní, on the other hand, have been able to avoid debt-bondage because, with food in the garden and forest, no family is forced to sell yerba cheaply, nor to buy trade goods at an inflated price. Patrons who drop the price they pay for yerba find that Guaraní collectors refuse to sell. Merchants who try to extract high prices for their goods, find that Guaraní consumers retreat into their gardens.

In fact, the economic independence of the Guaraní makes patrons cautious about lending to them. Since Guaraní do not need the economic support of the patron, it is possible for them to abscond from their debts. The merchant who provides food and equipment to a Guaraní family may find that they have abandoned their house and disappeared into the forest to join relatives elsewhere.

This is not to say that the Guaraní power in the marketplace is equal to patrons, or that Guaraní always avoid usurious debt. Merchants wield considerable influence in local communities. The patron seeking to collect on a debt to a Guaraní can depend on the full force of law and the brutal assistance of the local militia in punishing miscreants, if they can find them. Patrons also use their positions to artificially manipulate local economies. Paraguayan patrons have been known to dynamite bridges to control workers' access to markets.

Guaraní Consumption

Popular stereotypes suggest that indigenous peoples become enamored with new-found commodities from the world's bazaar, that people like the Guaraní put themselves innocently into lifelong debt for trinkets they do not need. This is not true of the Guaraní. When Avarijú goes to the market, he buys a few basic goods that he considers necessities. There are always more desires than money, and he weighs each choice against reasonable alternatives. After centuries of market experience, the Guaraní have learned to balance the purchase of a few things they cannot produce with their own subsistence production. The Guaraní market basket would be considered small and boring by most modern consumers. Food is the primary item, averaging about 40 percent of the average family's purchases. This includes a monthly average of about two kilos of rice, pasta and flour; a kilo of meat; and a half liter of cooking oil. Everyone buys a little salt, which is cheap and liked by all.

After food, cloth and clothing are the next most important purchases of Guaraní consumers. This gives a new shirt or pants (but probably not both) to most people every year. Soap, like salt, is purchased by all households. Guaraní consider personal hygiene a virtue and even the most tattered clothes are washed daily. The average family also spends about a fifth of its budget on tools, usually machetes, foice, and axes for subsistence agriculture. Finally, goods such as tobacco, tape recorders and alcohol, the stereotypical indigenous peoples' purchases, make up only a very small portion of the total expenditure. When Avarijú has paid for his necessities, he is lucky if a few cents remain for a piece of hardtack for the kids or tobacco leaf for himself.

Guaraní purchases provide useful goods that are not available in the forest. Salt, machetes and axes, medicines and soap have improved the lives of the Guaraní dramatically. None would be available if not for commercial markets. Even the polyester shirts, imported from Taiwan, wear far longer than the rough woven cotton that the Guaraní used to make themselves.

In addition, the market provides food when other sources of nutrition are unavailable. With the end of the corn harvest, farmers turn to pasta and rice from the market. Although hunting and fishing provide important protein, the marketplace provides a dependable (if expensive) source of meat. Just as subsistence production protects the Guaraní from total dependence on the commercial economy, the marketplace defends families against periodic shortfalls from hunting and horticulture.

In sum, the Guaraní have adapted their agroforestry to the environment of the tropical forests. They exploit a variety of ecological niches, and distribute their resource demands over time. The Guaraní have, thus, won a satisfying life from a fragile and infertile resource base.

The diverse economy of the Guaraní offers more than economic stability; it also provides social autonomy. By satisfying their basic needs from the forest, the Guaraní enter the market without becoming dependent on it. They retain the power to leave the commercial system and cut themselves off from Paraguayan society. Thus, the Guaraní have been a part of the market for four centuries without assimilating into the larger society.

4

Contemporary Development and Guaraní Communities

Flying over eastern Paraguay twenty years ago, I saw vast dark forests; the region appeared to be covered by a matting of thick green wool. Returning to the area today, one finds that much of that verdant cover has been cut, leaving the stubble and brown scars of a badly shorn sheep. Over the last two decades, vast areas of the deep forests have been felled for monocrop agriculture and cattle ranching. Traditional commercial gathering is being replaced by agriculture and ranching. These new production systems destroy the resource bases they depend on. Although clearing the forest provides short-term profits to entrepreneurs, it leaves a ravished landscape in its wake.

What is happening to Guaraní communities? Much of the Guaraní land has been drastically changed. Most of the trees are gone, and silt muddies the water. The small house lots that were once isolated in the forest are now exposed on the open landscape. The narrow footpath that led from Itanaramí to the nearby market town has been replaced by a road that moves heavy trucks across the hot landscape. New mestizo settlers are flooding into the area to build houses and clear fields. The cohesive and cooperative communities of a decade ago are being destroyed. Guaraní are abandoning their homes and kin to settle on the fringes of mestizo towns. Where the Spanish conquests could not conquer the Guaraní of the forest, the present changes are dispersing communities and assimilating their residents into the national society.

Why are indigenous communities destroyed by contemporary development? It is not simple contact with the larger system; the Guaraní have had relations with Europeans since the arrival of the Spanish. It is not even market involvement. Guaraní have sold commodities from the forest and purchased manufactured goods for centuries. This chapter shows that it is not market contact or interethnic relations that are destroying the Guaraní. Their society is being undermined by a new and unique type of economic development. For the first time in Guaraní history, outsiders are removing the forest and replacing it with totally new productive systems. This destroys both the forest and the Guaraní.

The following describes development in eastern Paraguay over the last twenty years. First, it shows the ecological damage wreaked by the recent economic and demographic expansion of the nation-state. Second, the chapter explores the government's efforts to settle the Guaraní on small reservations and replace their agroforestry with commercial agriculture. This policy toward the Guaraní, which seems pragmatic in the short-term, has devastating long range social and ecological consequences.

ECONOMIC DEVELOPMENT OR POLITICAL EXPEDIENCY?

After decades of little national economic growth, Paraguay experienced an annual expansion in the 1970s that averaged over 10 percent. In a continent of weak economies, Paraguay stood out as strong and vibrant, a force of the future. Paraguay's economic miracle was created by a spectacular expansion in agriculture. Fields of cotton, soy and wheat quickly became Paraguay's economic mainspring. By the 1990s, almost a quarter of the country's commercial production came from farming and ranching.

Increases in agricultural production in more industrial nations were created by technological innovations, such as bigger equipment and better fertilizers. Not so in Paraguay. The explosive growth of its agricultural sector was fueled by clearing new land. Almost half the land in eastern Paraguay is flat and dry enough to cultivate; almost all of it will grow some pasture. Since 1970, every effort has been made to convert as much of this land as possible into fields for commodity production. Forests were cleared in the farthest reaches of eastern Paraguay and roads cut to move commodities to national and international markets. However, these roads had as much to do with politics as economics, and the promised economic benefits have been overshadowed by a number of negative consequences.

Many of the first roads built into the eastern forests which spurred agricultural expansion were actually designed for military defense against the expansion of Brazil and Argentina. Paraguay has always had tenuous control of its small land area. With few mestizo settlers in the vast forests, the state has been unable to defend its eastern areas. Even with formal lines drawn, the last two decades have seen a migration of Brazilian settlers across the unprotected eastern border to settle and clear Paraguayan territory. Paraguay's long, dry border has also been vulnerable to international smuggling, and roads into these remote areas promoted the illegal flow of goods across the border. The military stationed along the border also facilitated smuggling, profiting from the illicit trade. This network of roads, partially financed with international aid from the U.S., was also used by the Paraguayan national police to root out peasant organizers and subdue rural uprisings (both real and imagined).

Despite the politics driving expansion into the forest, the subsistence needs of a burgeoning population was also a factor. Paraguay's population is concentrated around the capital city. As agriculture exhausted land in this central region, the government was forced to seek new territory. Rather than redistribute the fertile land that the wealthy manage as ranches and farms, the government enticed poor peasants into the forests with land distribution programs. Between 1963 and 1973, the Paraguayan government land agency, the Instituto

Bienestar Rural (IBR), distributed land to 42,000 families. This number more than doubled between 1973 and 1976, when IBR gave four million hectares to 48,000 peasant families. By 1984, roughly half the arable land in eastern Paraguay had been parceled out to Paraguayan colonists (UNESCO 1987:11).

International financial forces also pushed agriculture into the forest. After decades of resisting loans from private banks and multilateral lending agencies (such as the World Bank), Paraguay borrowed massive sums in the 1970s. In the most dramatic example, the government borrowed over a billion dollars to build hydroelectric dams on the Paraná River (Baer and Birch 1984:791). This infusion of financial capital generated profits that Paraguayan entrepreneurs needed to reinvest quickly. They used much of the easily earned money to build farms and ranches in tropical forests that have dubious long-term productivity.

Lenders demand that borrowers repay loans. While international capital was easily attracted to Paraguay, it was harder to repay. As the state's debt climbed, Paraguay sought rapid agricultural growth as a means to generate quick cash. The government provided cheap forested land to ranchers and agribusinesses, hoping that they would produce the exports to repay the international loans.

Although pragmatic in the short run, it is unclear that these investments are economically rational in the long term. On one hand, the development is uncontrolled, leading to waste of critical national resources. Second, the process expends the nation's greatest wealth, the forests and the soils, to underwrite Paraguay's wealthy elite and the national debt it has accumulated.

The problems created by international investment in development are clear in the case of a massive project called Proyecto Caazapa, in an area south of Itanaramí settled by Mbyá-Guaraní. Until recently, the rolling hills of Sierra de San Rafael were covered by dense forests and inhabited by scattered communities of Mbyá-Guaraní. The communities had effectively avoided direct contact with Paraguayan society by retreating into the deep forests. There, these Mbyá maintained their traditional political and religious leaders, the last being a powerful man named Juan Garay. Garay was a large man with a powerful presence, capable of unifying all Mbyá communities of Caazapa into a tight network.

As population pressure, ranching, and agriculture intensified near Asunción, Caazapa seemed a prime area for colonization and development. In 1983, the Paraguayan government proposed the site for an integrated rural development project funded by the World Bank. The state had more than a casual interest in the plan. The capital expended on road building, equipment and colonization would stimulate the flagging national economy.

The problems of this project provide fitting illustrations of the ecocidal and ethnocidal results of these development policies. The World Bank's efforts to help poor campesinos and indigenous peoples only exacerbated the problems faced by these groups. In addition, however, this case shows how anthropologists can work to protect indigenous groups affected by these types of projects.

Proyecto Caazapa was designed to move Paraguay's demographic and agricultural frontier through the forested hills of Caazapa toward the Brazilian border. Unfortunately, the Sierra de San Rafael was the last refuge of Mbyá Indians, who depended on the forests for gardens, hunting and yerba mate. The project was massive, including almost four hundred thousand hectares (almost fifteen thousand square miles). These forests were held by a variety of foreigners: Uruguayans, Swiss, Belgians, Argentines and Americans. Most had purchased large areas in the 1960s on speculation and had logged the valuable hardwoods for use in furniture and floors (Parquet 1985:114).

At a cost of fifty-four million dollars, principally from World Bank loans, the Paraguayan government built over four hundred kilometers of roads. These roads were designed to improve access, promote colonization and increase agricultural production in the last vast forests of southern Paraguay. The project provided credit and agricultural extension services for small farmers, and promoted the large-scale production of cotton and other cash crops.

Original plans for the project ignored the indigenous inhabitants of the region. Insituto Nacional del Indígena (INDI) estimated in 1979 that there were fewer than ten Mbyá families in the region, and suggested that their nomadic lifestyle made them difficult to locate (Fogel 1990). The INDI report was mistaken on the number of the Mbyá of Caazapa and their mode of living. In fact, there were seventeen Mbyá communities. INDI's ignorance was intentional. It gave new settlers *carte blanche* to clear the forests of the region.

Anthropologists had much to offer Proyecto Caazapa. First, anthropologists had traveled throughout the area long before the roads were built. They knew the location of each of the communities and had identified 730 families with over 3,800 Mbyá and Aché individuals. Anthropologists had talked with the Mbyá and learned that they wanted a single parcel of land large enough to hold all of their communities and leave sufficient forest for hunting and gathering. Second, anthropologists explained how the internal organization of Guaraní communities gave it a special need of forest. Not only did indigenous production depend on the sub-tropical ecosystem, but Guaraní identity depended on its relation to the forest.

When indigenistas and anthropologists pointed out the omissions of the INDI report, the World Bank stipulated that the final project proposal include an indigenous peoples component. This was to assure that the project not only defend the people, but benefit them. Indian lands were to be surveyed and titled to resident communities by 1984. The World Bank depended on the Paraguayan government to carry out the mandate. The agreement stipulated that loans be halted if the terms were not met for treatment of Indians.

Despite the World Bank mandate, 1984 passed without titling lands to the Mbyá. In fact, it took the Paraguayan government two years to initiate a census of the indigenous population within the region. That study specified the location and size of the Mbyá communities and the number of hectares necessary to satisfy the requirement of the Estatuto Indígena #904/81. It took no action to protect or title land for the indigenous people.

While little progress was made in the indigenous peoples component of Proyecto Caazapa, loans were dispersed for road building. By 1985, 230 kilometers of new and improved roads tied the most isolated areas of the forest into the national transportation systems. Colonists flowed into the area and commodities rolled out.

The project plan permitted logging only on farmland, but bulldozers quickly cut a network of logging roads into the steepest terrain. Colonists followed in the tracks cf the logging trucks and the landowners quickly exploited the newly created market for the land. They divided, surveyed and titled parcels to farmers for intensive commercial agriculture. Some settlers came from the overpopulated minifundias region to the west; others were brought as contrac: laborers from Brazil. They cut fields from the forest, strung fences and imported cattle. Soon the Mbyá communities were besieged by mestizo campesinos, Brazilian settlers, and Mennonite farmers.

Efforts to find a satisfactory solution to the problem suffered a severe blow in 1987, when the regional Mbyá political leader, Juan Garay, died. Garay's death left the dispersed Mbyá communities without a single voice. Moreover, the severe pressures created by Proyecto Caazapa prohibited the formation of new leadership alliances. The Mbyá remain without an effective leader to speak for the scattered and isolated groups.

The rush into Caazapa was exacerbated by the threat that land titles would be granted to indigenous residents. As the Mbyá had a legal claim to their lands, and the project had a component designed to satisfy those claims, private entrepreneurs worked quickly to exploit Mbyá forests before they were surveyed and mapped. When the national government finally moved to protect Indian land in 1987, it was devoid of the high forest that had been its greatest resource.

National and international criticism of Proyecto Caazapa forced the World Bank to suspend loans to Paraguay in 1987. What at first appeared a strong stand against the government proved an ineffectual, halfhearted move by the Bank. Loans were suspended after a major portion had been disbursed. This allowed the government to continue the road building for months before it needed further disbursements. The government quickly passed legislation (#1372/88) reiterating the 1981 Estatuto Indígena, once again codifying the specific steps for land titling. No land was titled to the indigenous communities and the World Bank quickly reinstated the loan with no lag in project activities.

When the government finally surveyed land in 1989, it was far less than necessary for the indigenous communities. Indigenistas estimate that six of the communities would need 40,000 hectares to protect them from economic and social dislocation (Rehnfeldt 1989:5). Only 7,200 hectares had been demarcated for these groups. Rather than satisfy the World Bank mandate to protect indigenous peoples, the Paraguayan government provided the legal minimum acreage due these communities, established under the Ley del Campesino for peasant farmers. As late as 1990, only one community in the region of Proyecto Caazapa had received title to its land. The remaining land remains in the hands of farmers, private corporations and INDI. Indians and indigenistas continue to fight for land, even as it is occupied by colonists and cleared for soybean fields and cattle ranches.

ECONOMIC EXPANSION OR ECOLOGICAL DESTRUCTION?

The forests of Itanaramí suffered their first serious incursion when the government cut a road from the south in 1972. This rough jeep track replaced the river as the economic and social link with the rest of the country. When weather was good, trucks filled with produce could trundle south to Asunción and north to the Brazilian border. This allowed the regional military commander to move troops and supplies through the area and gave him control over smuggling through the border into Brazil.

The road through the forests of Itanaramí also allowed logging in the previously impenetrable forests. Logging companies brought in heavy machinery that allowed loggers to comb upland forests for valuable hardwoods. Bulldozers cut paths to the base of each of the ancient trees. The trees were felled and dragged to the roads, where trucks carried them out of the forest. Sawyers from the United States built lumber mills along the new road. They trucked the cut lumber to the capital city, where it was loaded on boats for the United States, Japan and Argentina. The forests of Itanaramí, which have provided shelter and sustenance for this group for centuries, are being destroyed so that consumers around the world can enjoy beautiful furniture and parquet floors.

Settlers flowed into the Mbaracayú region on the new roads. The government established several colonization projects near Itanaramí. Lines were drawn on maps in government offices and surveyors cut trails across the unbroken forest. The vast forest was reduced to numbered plots and allotted to newcomers. Even without the benefit of land distribution programs, settlers followed the logging roads into isolated areas. Impoverished Paraguayan families trudged along the muddy roads, carrying their belongings on their backs. Once ensconced in the forest, they built thatch homes and cut fields illegally, hoping to legitimate their land claim eventually.

Besides the poor Paraguayans, truck loads of Brazilians arrived from the east. As land became scarce in southern Brazil, these Portuguese-speaking peasants sought cheap land and a better life in Paraguay. Brazilian patráos sold them transportation and rights to land in the Paraguayan forest. As three hundred thousand Brazilians flooded across the border, they came to outnumber native-born Paraguayans in many areas near Itanaramí.

Other kinds of settlers followed the roads into the forest. A large Mennonite colony settled near Itanaramí. Coming from Canada, Mexico and the United States, these religious pilgrims came to escape the problems and pressures of the more developed world. Many of these farmers recreated the lives they had left behind. Small farms, identical to those of Canada or United States, sprang up in the forest.

The social world of the Guaraní expanded dramatically as the wave of frontier settlement overran the area. A cacophony of Portuguese, Guaraní, Platt-Deutsch, and Spanish could be heard in the local town. Sunbonnets, straw hats and bib overalls filled the stores. Blacks, Europeans and mestizos mixed in the markets.

Quick on the heels of the new colonists, agrobusinesses found their way into the forest. Brazilian soybean producers and Paraguayan cotton growers came up the rough road in air-conditioned jeeps. With expensive sunglasses and leather brief cases in hand, these entrepreneurs stepped gingerly through the mud to stand at the edge of the forest beside the road and peer under the canopy. Although they quickly returned to the luxuries of Asunción, these men sent technical teams to test the soils, map the land, and plan their investments. Lawyers arrived with plat books and vast tracts of the forest were titled to faceless strangers in far off cities.

First, bulldozers ransacked the forest, widening logging tracks into avenues and stripping the forest cover from the land. The soft brown earth was exposed. The massive tractors were brought in to cultivate the soil and plant the crops. These new entrepreneurs generally opted to plant soybeans and wheat, avoiding traditional Paraguayan crops. Japanese firms developed hybrid grains that were planted in the reddish soil of the Guaraní forests. Within months of the entrepreneurs' arrival, the fields were covered with the pale green shoots.

Brazilian investors often avoided using expensive machinery. Instead, they imported land-hungry peasants from Brazil's overpopulated southwest. In Paraguay, poor peasants were given places to live by their patráo and allowed to clear forest for subsistence crops. At the end of each year, however, the Brazilians had to turn the cleared land over to the landowner and carve new fields from the forest. Although this process is slower than mechanized work, sometimes taking years to clear an area, it turns forest into field without the great expense of heavy equipment.

While farmers acquired the more fertile and well-drained land, ranchers bought poorer quality land for pasture. They felled the forest in river floodplains and slopes, planting imported grasses from Africa and Asia that flourished under the strong sun and rains. Ranching is ideal for entrepreneurs who wish to minimize investment in their land. Pasture reseeds itself for up to seven years, saving cultivation costs. Rather than use expensive improved stock, ranchers use local breeds that have survived generations on ranches elsewhere in Paraguay. Allowed to roam freely, this stock reproduces with little assistance, and ranchers cull saleable animals when they need cash.

Soon, the road that carried entrepreneurs' jeeps into the forest was plied by teetering truckloads of soybean and wheat. Alternately, the muddy track became the site of cattle drives, as vaqueros herded thousands of head to market. Where peasants came to the region to start a new life, the entrepreneurs arrived in search of profits. They won these profits in the short run, at a great expense to the tropical ecosystem and the people who had lived in it.

The economic expansion of the 1970s devastated the environment of eastern Paraguay. In the 1970s and 1980s, Paraguay's land was cleared faster than in any other country on the continent, as two frontiers advanced on the vast forests. Paraguayan peasants, military and entrepreneurs built roads and cleared land from the west. Brazilian farmers and ranchers spilled across the border from the east. The best farmland was cleared in the 1970s and, subsequently, the expansion continued apace into regions that were less suitable for cultivation.

Logging is the first foray of ecological destruction in the forest and damages the forest in fundamental ways. Flying over a newly logged area, the casual observer is likely to notice little change in the forest's environment. But the change is drastic and often irreversible.

Logging removes the highest canopy from the forest. The principal woods demanded by the international marketplace are dense hardwoods that are unique to tropical areas, such as *tajy´* (*Machaerium stipitatum*). Crowns of these trees are among the broadest of the forest. Although logging destroys only a small portion of the total tree species in the forest, these trees provide much of the protective cover.

The hardwood canopy contains a range of species that is hardly visible from the air or the ground. Vines spiral up trunks and create massive loops between the towering trees. Epiphytes, such as orchids (*Orquidaceas*) and philodendron (*Philodendron sellowianum*), dangle from branches, absorbing nutrients and moisture from the surrounding air and flora. Felling a very few hardwood species removes the primary pillars of this suspended ecosystem, dramatically diminishing the diversity of the original forest.

While logging has occurred in the forest for centuries, ecosystems survived. With the advent of contemporary technology and powerful equipment, ecosystems are being destroyed at a rate that was previously impossible. First, they permit commercial logging in areas that were previously inaccessible. Until 1970, oxen dragged logs to rivers, where they were floated downriver to mills. Logging activities were limited to areas within easy reach of navigable rivers. Heavy equipment now gives loggers access to the higher forests that are distant from major rivers. Floating bridges and immense culverts allowed roads to be cut directly south from Itanaramí to logging mills, avoiding the slow and tortuous river travel to the east.

Second, heavy equipment permits loggers to cut a network of roads in the forest. With bulldozers imported from the United States, logging trails can be made cheaply and quickly to each tree trunk. The logs are soon snaked down a maze of trails that wind through the undergrowth to the main roads. Cutting these trails destroys even more canopy than the felling of the forest giants. This vast network of unmarked and unmapped roads is ideal for squatters and colonists seeking access to the forests. Families follow the hundreds of trails that crisscross the forest, and the region becomes honeycombed by small clearings.

Third, heavy equipment allows developers to clear extensive tracts. After loggers remove valuable hardwoods, bulldozers push the remaining softwoods and undergrowth into long rows. After these tangles of stumps and vines dry, they are burned to a fine ash. The plumes of smoke hang heavy in the air, blocking the sun (and diverting plane flights) over the forest. When the fires fade, the reddish brown soil stands ready for the farmer or rancher. These fields often stretch several kilometers over the rolling hills, covering over ten thousand hectares (about four square miles). In some southeastern areas of Paraguay, it is now possible to drive many kilometers without passing a stand of trees.

Clearing from 1970 to 1976 reduced Paraguayan forests from 6.8 to 4.2 million hectares. Almost half the forests were cut by 1984. Five percent of the remaining forests are cut each year, as 150,000 to 200,000 hectares fall to axes and bulldozers (USAID 1985:128). This rate of clearing would remove all forests from Paraguay by 2020.

The destruction of the flora undermines the rest of the complex tropical ecosystem and destroys the extremely diverse fauna it harbors. It is estimated that three-quarters of all animal species live in the humid tropics, and most have been neither named nor described. The warm, wet forest is an ideal environment to incubate this diversity, allowing insects, spiders, mammals, fish and reptiles to evolve without extremes of environmental stresses.

Moving up from the forest floor, the biologist passes through various faunal strata. The beetles and moths of the understory are different from those of the first canopy and vary again in the upper canopy. Similarly, birds, mammals and other animal species adapt to the different forest micro-environments. Although there are many animal species, the populations are often small and scattered. A particular variety of beetle may be present in only one small area, or the population of giant armadillos spread very thinly over a broad area. This makes these animal species especially vulnerable to ecological disturbances.

Faunal populations begin to decline with the first harvesting of hardwoods in the forest. The insects, spiders and mammals that are adapted to the high canopy find their habitat greatly reduced. Some species dependent on specific trees are lost when logging decimates those plants. Destroying the canopy exposes forest animals adapted to the humid shade to the rigors of sunlight, heat and dryness.

Colonists create a second wave of faunal destruction. Settlers in the forest, whether Paraguayan or Brazilian farmers, supplement their gardens by hunting in the forest. Deer, peccary, and armadillos are favorite meats. In addition, colonists learn to eat new meats in the forest. They are soon avid hunters of tapir, paca, and capybara (*Hydrochoerus hydrochaeris*). Besides hunting for food, colonists kill animals for profit. Cats, fox (*Dusicyon gymnocercus*), and even lizards and caimans are sought for their valuable pelts and skins.

Hunting pressure is especially disruptive to fauna because it targets animals with population densities that are already low. Large mammals, such as tapir and deer, range widely through the forest but have small numbers. The removal of a few animals greatly affects the entire population throughout a large area. Commercial hunting is especially disturbing, as it focuses on animals near the top of the food chain. A few cats, foxes, or caiman (*Caiman latirostris* and *C. Crocodilus*) fill critical niches that regulate the populations of many species.

Habitat loss and hunting in the subtropical forests threatens six of Paraguay's seven species of wild cats (*Felis pardalis, F. tigrina, F. yaguaroundi, F. wiedii,* and *Panthera onca*) and animals as diverse as the tapir and giant armadillo (*Priodontes giganteus*). In addition, eleven species of birds and the caiman have been placed on the endangered species lists.

The removal of flora and fauna eliminates 90 percent of the forest ecosystem; the remaining 10 percent of nutrient value in subtropical zones is embedded in the forest soils. In the warm, moist shelter of the forest, bacteria rot the debris of fallen plants and dead animals. The decomposing life releases nutrients that other living organisms use. The sand and clay underlying tropical soils are poorer than more temperate soils, but provide a critical base into which trees can put down roots to find a few trace minerals and nutrients.

Harsh sun and direct rain strip the exposed soils of their fertility. As sunlight strikes the soils, temperatures rise dramatically. Where shaded ground often maintains a constant temperature of 75-80 degrees, sunlight quickly raises soil temperatures to over 100 degrees. Water trapped between the particles of soil and debris quickly evaporates. Bacteria die, stopping the process of nutrient release. As rainwater falls directly on the bare soil, it finds little to block its flow. Running off, it carries away the soil's remaining fertility. The brown sediment that once fertilized the forest muddies the streams and rivers.

As water washes nutrients away, it leaves behind the clay that lies beneath the surface. These clays lack fertility and are far too dense for tropical root systems. Moreover, these soils often harden into an impervious barrier when exposed to sunlight. Like a ceramic cap on the soil, this hardpan keeps seeds and water from entering the soils to restore the tropical ecosystem.

Land clearing for agriculture or ranching wields the final blow to the diversity of plant and animal diversity in the forest. Ranchers and agribusinesses bring new plant and animal life to supplant the old, but this new life is not diverse or sustainable. Monocrop agriculture; be it soybeans, wheat or cotton, depends on cultivating a single variety of one species, often plants that are genetically identical, over a wide area. Ranching attempts to create an ecosystem with only two residents, pasture and cattle. Ranchers exert great effort to limit the growth of other plants and animals in these regions.

Not only are new production systems genetically impoverished, they are often not sustainable. Intensive agriculture and ranching are adapted to more temperate climates. We have little information about the soils of eastern Paraguay and even less information about how weather and crops will change them. Despite its spectacular growth, the current economic development may be a short-lived phenomenon.

Agribusiness depends on crops that need constant care to reach maturity. The cotton that it cultivates, for example, dies at the end of the harvest season. In contrast, cotton grown by the Guaraní was harvested from a bush that survived the mild winters and did not need to be replanted. In addition, hybrid varieties need herbicide and insecticide, while indigenous cotton plants are disease and pest-resistant. (Agribusiness chooses hybrid varieties because the bolls mature at the same time, making them easier to harvest.)

Over the longer term, intensive agriculture and ranching rob the soil of nutrients necessary to sustain production. Cash crops, such as tobacco and cotton, make high demands for specific soil nutrients. But without the protection of the forest canopy, soils are quickly worn down and washed away. Commercial crops do well on new soils but fail as soils degrade. Even pasture, which grows with far fewer inputs and nutrient demands, needs to be replaced after five to seven years. Settlers, agribusinesses, and ranchers move farther into the forest as soil declines and hardpan forms. As they seek out new land and a fresh start, they leave a trail of environmental destruction behind.

The profits won from the first years of agriculture and ranching often blind producers to the long run implications of their activities. It is often possible to invest little and earn a profit before production declines. These short-term profits give the impression that production is economically rational. However, the profits are stolen from the environment, rather than earned by hard labor or investment.

In the region of Itanaramí, the land clearing has been even more rapid and dramatic. Large rivers protected the region from intensive development until the end of the 1970s. In 1972, the government estimated the population of Canindeyú at only 27,825 people. Even ten years later, the region remained the area of least population density in eastern Paraguay with 4.5 individuals per square kilometer. When all-weather roads were built into the region in the 1980s, it became the primary focus of logging, colonization and agribusiness development. In essence, the wave of frontier development struck Itanaramí and its forests in 1980.

The first incursion, as seen from the air, was the thin line that transversed the rolling forested hills, opening a narrow, reddish wound through the otherwise green forest. Brazilian colonists moved up from the south, opening a wedge in the forest by clearing both sides of the road. Soon a wide swath of pale green ran north to the Brazilian border.

Simultaneously, IBR began to organize large land distribution projects in the dense forests. Farmers cut branch roads into the green growth on both sides of the road to access their houses and gardens. Gardens quickly grew into large fields and the houses multiplied to become settlements.

Settlers to the region depended on commercial agriculture. In 1989, 63 percent of the farmers were producing cash crops, over three quarters grew cotton and the remaining tobacco. Colonists had access to considerable land, an average of over twenty hectares per family. Shortages of field labor, however, limited households to an average of 1.5 hectares of commercial crops. These recent arrivals' found farming profitable. Benefiting from the natural fertility of the soil and the nutrients of the recently burned forests, yields ranged from 40 to 55 percent greater than the national averages.

The development transformed the physical environment of Itanaramí. When I first arrived in the community in 1981, it was isolated in the forest. The mud and rivers forced me to walk eleven hours through the forest. As settlement progressed throughout the decade, my path was improved to a jeep track and then a logging road. The walk, which had been through the cool shade of the forest, was exposed to the harsh sun. Peasant families opened small farms along the road and cleared the cover of trees overhead. The damp soil became hot; dry sand and flies, rather than mosquitoes, hovered around me as I walked.

The development quickly arrived along the borders of Itanaramí. Mestizo squatters occupied and began to clear Itanaramí's eastern perimeter; IBR organized a settlement scheme to the west; a Mennonite colony began to clear the forests to the south. Then, in 1993, a ranch cut the forests to the north and constructed a road bisecting Itanaramí's land to provide access to forests on the far side the ranch. While the road itself did little environmental damage, it opened up a swath of the forest to colonization and commercial development. Houses sprang up along the route, and a small mestizo store opened inside the borders of the community. Mennonite loggers arrived in 1994 and bought the valuable timber that remained in the reserve, leaving behind only stacks of lumber from which the Guaraní built permanent, Brazilian-style houses. By 1995, Itanaramí was an island of forest in an ocean of agricultural fields.

DESTABILIZING GUARANÍ SOCIETY

The plight of indigenous people in developing areas has captured the attention of the larger world. Popular magazines display photos of native peoples in loincloths, standing beside immense yellow bulldozers. These people appear to be travelers from another time; they look out of place in the modern world. The images suggest that indigenous people are powerless and vulnerable in the face of the larger society.

We are left to believe that fragile indigenous cultures are torn apart by exposure to the harsh reality of the larger world.

The expansion of cattle ranching and intensive commercial agriculture into the forests has profound effects on the people who live in the forest. Besides destroying tropical ecosystems, these activities undermine the indigenous communities inhabiting them. However, bulldozers and money alone do not destroy indigenous society. We have seen that indigenous peoples in Paraguay and throughout the lowland forests have withstood decades, even centuries, of continual and often intense contact with the larger society.

A particular type of development is destroying indigenous communities. Intensive agriculture and ranching rob communities of land, forcing members into new productive activities. These new productive activities conflict with indigenous social institutions, dispersing groups and forcing individuals to assimilate into the larger society. The following details this economic change and points to its social and physical ramifications for indigenous people.

Economic Impacts

Development undermined the Guaraní economy first. As entrepreneurs arrived in Itanaramí, Avarijú watched surveyors plot lines through the forest. Narrow paths were cut along perfectly straight lines over hills and through swamps, imposing a new reality of private property on the land. Farmers cut clearings in the cool shade where he had hunted; built new houses along his old paths; and planted crops in his abandoned fields. These forces made the forest itself unfamiliar.

As the government sells land to private individuals, the new titles stipulate that the land be free of inhabitants. When new landowners take control of their property they feel a moral right and a legal prerogative to remove any people they find in the area. Guaraní discover that, with the stroke of a pen, they are squatters in their own homes.

Even when their houselots are not disturbed, Guaraní lose their forests. Traditional agroforestry exploited extensive tracts of forest. Each Guaraní community used tens of thousands of hectares of forest. Newcomers feel this forested land is underexploited. Intent on raising soybeans or cattle, few agribusinesses understand the complex and subtle ways that Guaraní make use of all ecological niches. They assume that standing forests are unused and that indigenous residents need to make room for developers who will use the resources.

As Guaraní lands are sold to developers, they are forced onto progressively smaller parcels. The refugees seek out a corner of the forest that remains untitled or, if fortunate, hold onto their houses and fields. Moreover, newcomers demand and develop the lands that the Guaraní use most intensely. Agribusiness prefers well-drained parcels with high canopy forests; settlers seek out springs and other sources of water. Thus, beyond being forced onto small parcels, Guaraní lose the most desirable locations for communities and gardens.

Guaraní hunting is one of the first productive activities affected by colonization and forest clearing. Newcomers destroy both the populations and habitat of Guaraní game animals. As mentioned, hunting quickly destroys large game populations and reduces the number of smaller animals as well. The process is exacerbated by habitat loss. Even where some stands of high forest remain, clearing divides extensive tracts of forest and makes it difficult for peccary, deer and tapir to roam over large areas. Colonists clear stream banks and brushy thickets, which are the prime habitat for small animals. Even bird populations come under attack. The Guaraní found that the large ground birds, the turkeys of the forest, were quickly shot off by settlers.

As game animals are destroyed, the Guaraní lose critical protein in their diet. Leaving for the hunt in the morning, Avarijú found his hunting territory increasingly restricted. Settlers cut fields into one of his favorite hunting areas; a rancher strung a barbed wire fence across the path to another hunting spot; and the *encargado* who managed a third location bought a mean dog to keep people out.

Where meat from the forest could previously compensate for the annual decline in garden production, now there was no cushion from the karuvaí. When hunters return empty-handed, the family is forced to look elsewhere for meat. In

Itanaramí, this meant looking to commercial markets. The ranchers who cut the forest provided a ready source of beef. Each morning they slaughtered a cow or steer in town, providing Avarijú and his relatives meat to fill the family pot - if they had cash. In essence, the beef was produced on the land that had provided peccary or armadillo meat. Now, however, the Guaraní needed to offer cash to a *latifundista*, a large landowner, to get access to it.

The loss of the forest also undermines the commercial portion of the Guaraní economy. Developers cut the trees that produce valuable foliage, oils and timber. The first resources to disappear are the forest animals with valuable pelts. The loss of deer and peccary not only reduces protein in the Guaraní diet, but it robs the Guaraní of the wealth won from the sale of their skins. In addition, wild cats and foxes prefer the solitude of deep woods. They disappear as the colonists' fields transect the forests.

Development also destroys tree crops that the Guaraní have cultivated over five centuries. As ranchers and farmers clear the forest for planting, they destroy the stands of yerba mate and citrus trees. The Guaraní do not even profit from labor in logging. Previous logging activities demanded human labor to seek, fell and transport timber, but the present lumber industry replaces workers with machinery imported from more developed countries.

As we learn about the forest environment, we discover that seemingly insignificant changes have far reaching ecological effects. For example, large ground birds, called *jacú* (*Aburria jacutinga*), are a favorite quarry of new settlers, since they provide up to two kilos of meat. Jacú were quickly killed off by the new settlers in the region of Itanaramí. The declining population of jacú was bothersome to the Guaraní, as they were a good source of protein, but more serious were the secondary effects of the hunting; it inhibited the germination of yerba seedlings. Yerba seeds have a tough exterior shell that needs to be broken for the plant to germinate. When the jacú eats the yerba berry, the grit and acid of the bird's digestive track weaken the seed's hard exocarp. Destroying these game birds greatly affects the Guaraní yerba production.

As Guaraní lose cash income from commercial extraction, they look for other ways to buy the goods they need. Some hire themselves out as fieldhands to the new commercial farmers of the region. Others become cash croppers themselves. These new endeavors, however, limit their choices and undermine indigenous communities.

As the people of Itanaramí lost their forest, they switched to commercial agriculture with enthusiasm. Fields of cotton and tobacco sprout beside the houses of the new settlers and, at harvest, oxcarts laden with produce trundle off to market in town and return laden with bags of beans and boxes of clothes. The Guaraní attempt to emulate the settlers' apparent easy access to money and goods. Moreover, government assistance programs promote commercial agriculture by indigenous peoples. Agronomists and technicians arrive in Guaraní communities with seed, pesticide and sprayers, delivering spirited lectures about the opportunities of commercial farming. Soon all of the Guaraní were clearing land for cotton, planning excitedly how they were going to spend their cash.

In Itanaramí, the grim realities of commercial agriculture were evident even before they harvested the first crops. Unlike the previous diversified production system, which assured food and income throughout the year, commercial agriculture provides a single product at the end of the harvest. A family's needs, however, are constant and diverse.

Farmers had no food during the long growing season. A man working in his cotton field does not have the time or energy to go fishing or hunting, even if forest is available. He may not even have time to plant a food garden. Therefore, cotton farmers needed to buy meat, rice, salt and other basic foodstuffs. Farming families also have household needs. Purchases of machetes, axes, shirts and blouses cannot wait until cotton bolls are mature. Finally, commercial farming, itself, demands capital inputs. Cotton and tobacco need to be protected with herbicide and insecticide, and next year's seed cannot be saved from last year's harvest. Commercial crops are very vulnerable to damage, and if weevils infest the cotton bolls, the farmer's entire year's income is lost. Farmers need to take all steps possible to protect their plants. These manufactured products are imported from Brazil, Japan, and the United States and are expensive.

Guaraní commercial farmers are forced to go into debt to support their families until they harvest the crop. After centuries of avoiding credit, Guaraní find that the new production regime forces them to borrow money from a local merchant. Store owners are only too eager to extend credit, providing food, clothing or tools to cotton farmers.

This credit, however, limits the power of Guaraní as purchasers. They can no longer haggle over prices. When a family buys rice on credit, the price is fixed. Merchants are unwilling to throw an extra scoopful into the bag or knock a little off the price. Food on credit may even cost a little more, ostensibly to cover interest and the merchants' risk. Once Guaraní cotton farmers accept credit from one merchant they find other store owners reluctant to sell to them. Sellers prefer to work with debtors who have unencumbered loyalties, and merchants avoid buyers who are in debt elsewhere. Thus, buyers are forced to pay the inflated prices of the merchant who gives them credit.

Commercial farming allows much higher debt loads on Guaraní producers. Mestizo lenders previously avoided large loans, fearing that Guaraní would abscond on their debts. The crop in the field becomes the lender's collateral. The field guarantees that the farmer will not disappear into the forest. If a family escapes to Brazil, they must abandon their cotton, and the merchant will use it to cover their debt.

Credit also restricts commercial farmers' power as a seller. Loans are usually extended by a merchant on the condition that the Guaraní will market their crops through that store. When the time comes to market the crop, farmers must accept the price that the store owner sets. This figure is usually several percentage points below the local market rate. Thus, as Guaraní enter commercial farming, they become locked into market relations that transfer a portion of their production (and income) to merchants. Farmers often discover that the money they earn covers only their debt, leaving no profit to buy goods in preparation for the next agricultural year.

Local merchants often use direct force to gain even greater control over regional commodity markets. Police and military officials in small towns sometimes collaborate with local cotton and tobacco merchants. They may jail farmers who refuse to sell the crop at a creditor's price or harass merchants who come from other areas to buy cotton. One powerful local store owner in eastern Paraguay dynamited the roads, leaving only one route that passed through his land. All producers had to market their crop through him, and accept the low prices he offered.

Finally, commercial agriculture is very risky. Insects and weather could destroy the crop before harvest; bad roads could prevent it from reaching market; or price manipulations might render the crop worthless. A farmer could toil for a year in the hot sun and discover that he has no income, and has fallen deep in debt to his patron.

While some become cotton farmers, other people of Itanaramí are turning to wage labor. Wage labor offers a less risky means of earning cash. As Avarijú picks up his machete and heads off to his tobacco field, his brother-in-law, Avaver, might take his hoe and go to the house of his mestizo patron. Avaverá will toil through the day weeding cotton or planting pasture, and return home with cash in his pocket. The Guaraní who chooses to spend the day hoeing tobacco or picking cotton in someone else's field, is guaranteed a set amount of cash for his efforts. In effect, day laborers accept none of the risk shouldered by commercial producers.

Field labor has several serious disadvantages for Guaraní workers, however. First, employers pay field hands low wages. The cash earned in a day might buy a kilo of meat or two liters of oil, but not enough to support a family. A family that wishes to provide for itself with day labor must send several, often all, of its members into the fields. Second, workers are often forced to travel and live outside their communities to find work. The largest employers live several hours' walk from Guaraní communities. Living in temporary, often uncomfortable shelters at the worksite, the Guaraní are vulnerable to harassment by non-Indians. Since they are separated from their gardens, Guaraní workers spend most of their income to buy food from their patron and have little to carry back to their villages.

Commercial agriculture and wage labor offer Guaraní means to replace cash that is no longer available from gathering forest commodities. But these activities drain indigenous communities of precious resources. First, commercial agriculture forces Guaraní to increase the rate that they cut down their own forests. Cotton and tobacco farmers plant two gardens each year: one for food and another for cash. As the rest of the region is cleared by outsiders, the Guaraní destroy the limited forests they control at an alarming rate. A survey of commercial farmers in Itanaramí shows that commercial cultivators clear almost twice as much land as Guaraní subsistence farmers. Second, wage labor demands the strongest workers. Labor resources in the community are greatly diminished as young, male workers travel off to work on ranches and farms in distant zones. Older and female workers are left behind and find it difficult to perform the laborious task of clearing fields for planting. They become dependent on markets, spending their husbands' wages to buy food.

Health Impacts

The economic decline of commercial gathering has serious health ramifications in Guaraní communities. As food becomes scarce, hunger undermines the resistance of indigenous people to disease. Poor nutrition makes them susceptible to illnesses, such as colds, tuberculosis and flu.

Visitors to Guaraní communities often find the entire population beset by a common ailment. Periodic epidemics of measles and chicken pox wipe out large portions of the population. The infant mortality rate of the Guaraní hovers around 25 percent; almost a quarter of the population dies before it reaches five years old (INDI 1982). This susceptibility of indigenous people to illness had been attributed to an absence of immunities that protect other populations. Recent research, however, suggests that social and ecological pressures rather than genetic defects make indigenous people susceptible to illness. This is not to say that genetics is not a factor at all. Having descended from a handful of migrants from the north, South American indigenous peoples do have a similar genetic blueprint, which facilitates the transmission of illness from one individual to the next.

Once a disease is contracted, however, social factors exacerbate the symptoms and increase the likelihood of death. We can only understand the health problems of the Guaraní in the context of the population's economic hardships. As protein in the community declines, families are forced to subsist on a diet that is higher in fats and starches. A wage laborer commonly breakfasts on fried manioc flour. His children might get only boiled manioc. These empty calories provide few of the resources that are necessary to fend off bacteria and viruses.

Given the ease of transmission of illnesses, increasing population densities exacerbate the health problems of the Guaraní. When indigenous people were dispersed throughout the forest, there was little opportunity to pass infections between people. Today, forced onto smaller parcels with houses near one another, the water the Guaraní drink and the air they breathe is laden with microbes and parasites. As mestizos and Brazilians flood into the forest, each new wave of flu and colds quickly finds its way from the capital city into the forest, bringing disease to the previously isolated Guaraní.

The stress of economic insecurity also increases indigenous health problems. As resources become scarce and production problems grow, new types of personal and social problems rise. Economic displacement increases individuals' tension and fears. This stress not only diminishes immunological functioning, but it increases alcoholism and domestic abuse, as well as violence between families and by mestizos against Guaraní. Most alarmingly, recent years have seen a dramatic increase in suicide rates among Guaraní in deforested areas.

Wage labor and commercial farming lead to other health problems as well. Powerful insecticides come to rural farmers with few instructions and cautions. Pesticides are often stored near food and applied carelessly; any extra is spread on the skin to kill parasites; and empty canisters are recycled as water containers or children's toys. There are no controlled studies to judge the effects of this pesticide poisoning among Guaraní, but serious neurological and congenital problems have become evident among mestizo cotton growers. Indigenous peoples are undoubtedly suffering as well.

Guaraní health problems are exacerbated when indigenous curing systems are undermined by national health systems. Sick Guaraní need family and friends to tend their gardens or to go for medicine. Migrant workers find themselves without these social networks. They must fend for themselves, scavenging food and medicine to regain health. Even in established communities, epidemics can overwhelm support networks. When all residents are debilitated by the flu or chicken pox, gardens go unplanted, food goes uncooked, and animals are untended. Without medicine and help, many more sick will die.

Guaraní health problems extend into the psychological sphere. Suicide has increased dramatically in Guaraní communities. The rise was first identified in the Brazilian state of Mato Grosso do Sul, across the border from Itanaramí. There has been a steady increase in suicide over the last years, from 6 suicides recorded in 1989 to an average of over 3 suicides per month in the first half of 1995. These figures only include the successful suicides; there are at least twice as many unsuccessful attempts. The rate of suicides among Paraguayan Guaraní have begun to increase as well (Meliá 1995:30).

The suicide rate among the Guaraní is being exacerbated by the recent economic pressures of the Guaraní. Individuals are powerless in the face of the new economy and become vulnerable to depression and suicide. It is not coincidental that the suicide rate is highest among young adults, who are finding it increasingly difficult to establish themselves in the new economic order.

In sum, the health problems that accost indigenous people in developing areas must be understood in their social context. Declining nutrition, social conflict, and personal isolation exacerbate minor health concerns.

Social Impacts

The economic changes in eastern Paraguay are transforming indigenous social institutions. As Guaraní forge new political relations with mestizos, traditional relations within indigenous society are disrupted. The distinct organization and ethnic identity which has been retained over centuries of contact with European colonists and mestizo settlers is now being threatened by contemporary development.

As discussed in the second chapter, Guaraní communities are organized around kin leaders. As children grow and marry, they settle near their parents. Older family members become the organizing force for larger residence groups, providing the central node of kin networks that are the basic structure of Guaraní communities. They make decisions for the group and mediate disputes between their progeny and relatives. These kin leaders legitimate their position of power through reference to religious knowledge. Meditation and prayer allow kin leaders to develop close relations with supernatural beings and, as poraéa, they mediate relations between the deities and the group.

Poraéa lose influence as farmers increase economic ties outside the community. Although kin leaders may mediate between Guaraní individuals and the supernatural, they lack the knowledge and power to mediate relations between the Guaraní and the larger system. They are powerless to garner more credit for the needy farmer or to protect land from surveyors and loggers. Kin leaders cannot mediate disputes of Guaraní farmers with merchants or government bureaucrats.

New political leaders are appearing in Guaraní communities. They become more powerful, even as traditional kin leaders lose standing. These political leaders develop the means to mediate the increasingly complicated ties between the Guaraní and the larger society. *Caciques*, a label borrowed from the Incas, are appointed by the national government. They are given identification cards and empowered by the state to speak for the entire community. Recognized by mestizos as Guaraní leaders, caciques mediate land conflicts, deal with local police, and facilitate assistance projects.

A primary purpose of caciques has been to legitimize the removal of Guaraní from their lands. In exchange for the thousands of square kilometers that the government took from Guaraní, the government offered small plots with a few hundreds of hectares. To legitimize this transfer, the government needed an official representative of the Guaraní. Ostensibly, the cacique is supposed to help the community, reading and signing the documents that ratify the exchange for the Guaraní. Instead, they merely appease them.

Once recognized by the government, caciques serve a host of other functions at the regional and national level. Local police appeal to them to help enforce the government's laws. Merchants look to them for help in getting loans repaid. Mestizo cotton and tobacco farmers ask them for field hands to harvest their crops. Political bosses turn to the caciques to get the vote out for the favorite candidates. In effect, the cacique becomes the broker between the Guaraní community and the larger society.

Assistance programs have been a principal source of power for caciques. International aid projects, missionaries, and government programs all seek to provide aid to the Guaraní. As caciques ostensibly represent their communities and are comfortable associating with non-Guaraní, they become a prime contact between these assistance agencies and the Guaraní. Caciques define the needs of the group to these agencies and become the primary means through which benefits flow to the group. In Itanaramí, for example, international aid was sent to help Guaraní plant cotton. The cacique distributed the seed, tools and pesticide to community residents as if it were a gift from him. When the agency provided cash to help producers avoid debt until harvest, the cacique made decisions about who received what amounts. His close friends and family benefited greatly, his more distant kin and political foes fared poorly.

Traditional leadership, in the form of the poraéa, is based in kin connections and religious knowledge, and wields influence, not power. Poraéa have no means to coerce their followers. Caciques' power, in contrast, derives from association with institutions outside the community. When the cacique of Itanaramí distributed cotton assistance, he created a relationship with individuals that had many features of mestizo patronage. He suggested that the recipients were responsible for returning the profits from their cotton fields to him, and would remain in his debt until they did so.

When a cacique brokers a land claim, he wields some of the power that the government asserts over resources. When a cacique turns a wayward debtor over to a merchant, he becomes party to the economic power of that lender. When a cacique distributes assistance or helps administer an aid program, the recipients in turn owe him a favor. In short, unlike the poraéa who depends on respect and trust to influence behavior, the cacique can assert his will, even when he and his decisions are unpopular. He has the power of the police, the military, even international aid agencies behind him.

As interethnic ties empower new political leaders, kin networks that defined Guaraní communities are breaking down. Previously, Guaraní communities were loosely linked networks of kin who resided in the same general area. Membership was fluid, changing often as nuclear families shifted periodically among various groups. Today, the national government defines Guaraní communities as demarcated zones, and their memberships are fixed in national censuses. Officials of the Instituto Nacional del Indígena (INDI), the national agency of indigenous peoples, list members in their registers in the capital city.

The search for new resources has forced many nuclear families to abandon their Guaraní kin networks and move into Paraguayan mestizo society. Cotton farmers can get more credit if they offer a land title as collateral. To get personal titles, families often leave Itanaramí and apply directly to the national land agency for a plot in an area of colonization. They build homes near Paraguayan campesinos and quietly insinuate themselves into mestizo society.

Other Guaraní abandon Itanaramí in search of wage labor. Young men and their families often travel several days in search of work, walking along forest paths or dusty roads to a Mennonite farm or Brazilian *fazenda*. Some Guaraní make their way two hundred kilometers into the capital city. In the past these itinerant laborers returned to Itanaramí and reintegrated themselves into community networks. A growing

number, however, find it economically advantageous to remain in mestizo society. Since no commercial gathering can
be done near Itanaramí, they stay where wage work is available. These families set themselves up in hovels and home-
steads near their employers and are eventually lost to their
friends and family in the Guaraní community.

In sum, the expansion of intensive farming and cattle
ranching into Guaraní forests has disrupted indigenous society to a greater extent than the previous four centuries of interethnic contact. The loss of land has serious ramifications
for Guaraní economy, health and social organization. The
felling of the forest begins a process in which Guaraní economic production is undermined, Guaraní health is debilitated, and Guaraní society adopts the internal power relations
of the hierarchical system. Even as Guaraní communities are
being mapped and platted, their populations are dispersing
and their members assimilating into the larger system.

DISLOCATING GUARANÍ COMMUNITIES

Most Guaraní communities have been relocated at least once
by this development. Many have been forced to move several
times. The case of Ñandurocaí illustrates the process by
which families are torn from their gardens and homes, often
violently, and forced to search out new places to live in the
diminishing forest. The community now is located north of
the town of Igatimí. Since the arrival of the Spanish in the
16th century, the Guaraní have lived and worked in the hilly
forests that mark the present Paraguayan border with Brazil.
In the northern regions of the Department of Canindeyú
these hills are known as the *Sierra de Mbaracayú*. In addition
to the high canopy of hardwoods that cover the hills, the forests along rivers and streams hold the densest growths of
yerba mate throughout the region.

Yerba has been harvested from the forests of Mbaracayú
since the first years of the conquest. Spanish conquistadors
ascended the Jejuí River into Mbaracayú and began to produce yerba with Guaraní labor. Throughout the eighteenth
and nineteenth centuries, groups of Guaraní and mestizos
continued to harvest the yerbales of Mbaracayú, shipping

enormous bales of the leaf downriver to Asunción and Buenos Aires. In the early years of the twentieth century, the yerba of Mbaracayú provided the profits for the development of Paraguay's largest corporation, La Industrial Paraguaya. The latifundista produced many of the forest commodities that drove the national economy.

Until the 1970s, the Guaraní lived in relative peace in the forests of Mbaracayú. Several large populations lived in stable communities, places with names like Ñandurocaí and Yvypyt. Families collected yerba and sold it to La Industrial, gardened and trapped game in the fertile forests, and fished the abundant streams. Far from the centers of mestizo settlement and commerce, they could ensconce themselves in the forest and control their relations with the larger society. In 1972, the government sold the forests of Mbaracayú to entrepreneurs who were primarily interested in turning a quick profit. The hills were surveyed and titled, and the resources were inventoried. Timber was a prime asset of the land. The high canopy was a dense growth of valuable hardwoods destined to be lumber for parquet floors and furniture in the United States. A single investor purchased one vast area of 50,000 hectares. This man, a Paraguayan of Italian descent, had earned tremendous wealth in lumbering nearer the capital city. Soon roads were cut into the heart of the region and logging trucks were ripping the best of the timber from the land. As the border was poorly patrolled and prices were higher in Brazil, the loggers sold their timber across the border.

Guaraní communities of Mbaracayú were disturbed by the loggers who invaded the forests. An encargado, hired by the logging company to manage the land, became the single and ultimate authority of the region. The Paraguayan police have never provided much protection for indigenous peoples, and the government's law has little power in the forest. The sullen, dirty loggers acted with impunity when they strolled into Ñandurocaí and the other Guaraní communities. They took food from gardens and meat from hunters. Guaraní women were raped. The administrator considered it a favor that he allowed the indigenous people to even remain on the land. Native communities were forced to move farther into the forest as logging approached; Guaraní moved furtively on paths in the forest.

When much of the valuable hardwood had been removed, the logging company went bankrupt. The World Bank, which had taken the land as collateral on a loan, foreclosed on the property. Before the bank took possession, however, the manager forced all remaining Guaraní outside the borders of the property. He explained that he had allowed them to stay, but could no longer extend that charity under the new ownership. Those who delayed their move found their homes were burned and their gardens plundered. They were forced to begin a new life, cutting new gardens and building new homes outside Mbaracayú.

When the bank took control of the land, it was effectively without residents. The new manager restricted all Guaraní activities in the area. They were not allowed to collect yerba, hunt, trap or fish. When hunters ventured into Mbaracayú, they were subject to brutal punishments.

In one instance, six Guaraní men were discovered cutting yerba in an isolated portion of the land. The men describe how they were bound at gunpoint and transported to an adobe building at the edge of the property. They were locked for a month in a room that measured eight by twelve feet, ostensibly while the police were being summoned. Cold manioc and water were passed to them once each day. The captives were forced to relieve themselves in a corner of the room, fouling the floor with their own excrement. After thirty days, the men were dehydrated, sick and malnourished. They were finally released without any formal action to walk the forty miles back to their community and report the dangers of trespassing.

When they were evicted from Mbaracayú, many Guaraní resettled in a grassy plain called Ñandurocaí on the edge of the property. This site provided good water from a nearby stream, fertile land for gardens, and was near other communities where most of the migrants had close relatives. Being a good place for farming, Ñandurocaí quickly attracted mestizo settlers as well. These poor farmers came into the forest along the new road and built homes and planted fields on the grassy plain.

The mestizos and Guaraní lived peaceably for several years. The newcomers befriended the Guaraní and benefited from the indigenous residents' knowledge of the region. As the number of mestizo settlers in Ñandurocaí increased, however, the tenuous alliance broke down. Small frictions grew into larger conflicts. A pig invaded a garden. A machete was stolen. One night, after several mestizo men had been drinking, there was a fight, and a Guaraní man was severely beaten. After that, the Guaraní lived in fear for their homes, their families and their gardens. Rather than risk another confrontation, the indigenous residents quietly moved farther from Mbaracayú.

The Guaraní of Ñandurocaí found their third community site at the confluence of two rivers, within an hour's walk of Ñandurocaí. They again cut gardens and built homes. This time, however, they appealed to the federal agency of indigenous people to protect their land as a Colonia Nacional Indígena. Pooling their resources, they sent a representative to Asunción to present their petition for fifteen hundred hectares of the land they now occupied. Within weeks, a military official visited the site and assured them that the land they wanted would be theirs. Surveying teams were dispatched to plot the region and cut boundaries through the forest.

Unfortunately, when the government delivered a map to the Guaraní, the land measured less than half that requested in their original petition. They discovered that the helpful military officer who had facilitated their land claim had received title to the other eight hundred hectares they were expecting. He was dividing it and reselling it to mestizo colonists. The Guaraní could have fought for their land, but they risked angering the military and losing the smaller parcel they were given. For the third time in a decade, this community stood by, powerless to stop the steady erosion of their territory.

GUARANÍ SOCIETY AND ASSISTANCE PROGRAMS

The plight of the Guaraní has not gone unnoticed; a variety of public and private agencies have attempted to help them. Evangelical missionaries, government bureaucracies, anthropologists, and indigenous peoples' rights activists have interceded in their behalf. Each of these groups has an agenda of its own, however, often with little understanding of the needs and the desires of the Guaraní themselves.

Missionaries were among the first groups to work with the Guaraní. In the 1930s, evangelists arrived from Germany to proselytize in the forests of eastern Paraguay. Building churches in the forest, Christian pastors attempted to win the souls of the Guaraní. They had little success, however. The few Guaraní neophytes attracted to churches generally abandoned their newfound religion when the missionaries moved on. Recently, missionaries have turned their attention from Bibles to development and attempted to help the Guaraní cope with rapid change. They brought new crops and built sanitation centers, even providing some communities with electricity for lights and radios. These efforts have hastened Guaraní integration into Paraguayan society rather than promoting indigenous power and independence. Missionaries, like development agencies, introduce the Guaraní to commercial farming without providing resources needed for the Guaraní to be independent nor the tools to compete in the economic mainstream.

Until the 1960s, the government's relations with indigenous groups were primarily through the military. Until the 1930s, the Paraguayan government had only tenuous control over its land. The government considered indigenous groups a threat to national security. When the military encountered indigenous groups, it used force to "pacify" them. Guaraní did their best to avoid this contact. They ensconced themselves in the forests of large landowners and gathered goods for sale, out of the reach of the national government.

These isolated Guaraní communities came to the attention of government bureaucrats in the 1960s, when the government began to expropriate the land of the latifundistas.

Rather than the Guaraní being feared as a military threat, they were now pitied as culturally inferior. (In fact, most Paraguayans considered indigenous people less than human, primarily because they had not converted to Catholicism [Chase-Sardi 1973:78].) Government officials saw Guaraní gardening and hunting as evidence of their economic backwardness. The solution to what they called "the Indian problem" was to assimilate the Guaraní into the national society.

As the Guaraní moved from being a physical threat to a social problem, the military established an office to manage the population. The Departmento Asuntos Indígenas (DAI) set out to help the Guaraní abandon their so-called "primitive past" and move into the "modern world." The DAI distributed seeds in Guaraní communities and government agronomists gave lectures on the benefits of commercial agriculture. A few of the Guaraní tried cotton and tobacco, but the work was hard, the debts were dangerous, and any profits were meager. Most of them abandoned cash cropping when government supports stopped; there was little incentive to leave the stability of commercial agroforestry. DAI degenerated quickly into a feeding trough for political appointees who fattened themselves on the paltry sums allocated to help indigenous people.

In the 1970s, the military created a new agency to deal with their problem with indigenous people. Rather than simply promote assimilation, the Instituto Nacional del Indígena (INDI) tried to defend the indigenous population in the transition to modernity. Its most important task was to reserve and protect land for the Guaraní. As ranchers and farmers divided eastern Paraguay into lots and cleared the forest, INDI surveyed and reserved land for indigenous communities.

The government effort to title land to Guaraní moved quickly in the 1970s. Over half the indigenous residents of eastern Paraguay had some land by the end of the decade. This demarcation slowed, however, as private developers acquired the last of the public land in the region. By 1995, approximately 1,100 Guaraní remained without land. Representing a fifth of the total Guaraní population, most of these people were Mbyá -Guaraní who were dispersed in the remaining forests.

Beginning in 1983, the government issued titles to indigenous communities. These titles are held in common and cannot be sold or used as collateral. Although these programs offered some land to many Guaraní, they failed to provide them the area necessary to continue as an independent ethnic group. Land is titled to Guaraní under the guidelines established for mestizo peasants, twenty hectares to each family. This may be sufficient for commercial cropping, but it is not enough land for commercial agroforestry. Moreover, INDI made no effort to give Guaraní access to the yerba that had previously provided for their cash needs.

Worse still, many lands are titled to Guaraní only after the timber has been cleared. In some cases, private loggers strip public land before the government secures it for indigenous residents. Even rumors that a parcel will be titled to indigenous residents create a feeding frenzy of timber buyers who cart off the timber before officials complete the necessary paperwork. Often, it is government bureaucrats themselves who contract for the sale of the lumber. Corrupt officials sell reservation timber as a kickback for titling land to the Guaraní. The land the Guaraní receive is barren, suitable only for farming and ranching.

INDI's land program fulfills the agency's previous objective. It assimilates the indigenous population into commercial agriculture and peasant society. Officials recognized the success of this effort in 1993, when INDI moved from the Ministry of Defense to the Ministry of Agriculture and Ranching.

The Guaraní have received considerable aid from private sources. In the 1970s, the deteriorating conditions of the Guaraní came to the attention of the academics and human rights activists. Foreign anthropologists who had lived in indigenous communities pressured the Paraguayan government to give land to Indians. Paraguayan human rights activists called international attention to the state of the native groups. The case was quickly taken up by international indigenous peoples' rights groups, such as Cultural Survival and Survival International.

Paraguayan activists began to work with indigenous communities to promote self-sufficiency and self-determination. With funding from international sources, these *indigenistas* attacked the various problems besetting indigenous communities. Technicians, health workers and community organizers fanned out into the rural areas to visit indigenous communities, discover their problems, and work with them to find solutions. Health has been a principal concern of indigenous assistance groups. Funded by the Swiss Red Cross, Paraguayan health workers opened a small clinic where Guaraní patients could come with their families. Teams of doctors visited communities, vaccinating children against and dispensing medicines for the chronic sicknesses of adults.

Private assistance groups also provided the Guaraní with the resources for commercial agricultural. Seed and technicians arrived in the Guaraní communities with rotating credit funds to free producers up from dependence on exploitative merchants.

Finally, private assistance groups have strengthened internal social networks among indigenous peoples so they can work effectively to defend themselves and determine their future. Until 1989, the Paraguayan government controlled political parties and outlawed unions. Nevertheless, activists organized federations of indigenous communities. They brought together representatives from each community to meet with others of their ethnic group. Thus, Chiripá representatives met among themselves; Pai-tavyterá leaders organized their own group; and Mbyá leaders formed yet a third. Meetings were held in indigenous communities, where there were fewer intrusions of Paraguayan national society. Participants in these meetings emphasized Guaraní norms of behavior. In one of these meetings in Itanaramí, members arrived on foot from the various nearby communities. Most stayed in the homes of relatives during the several days it took to reach an accord. When time came for meetings, the entire group assembled in a large circle near the religious leaders house. There was no agenda, but discussion eventually moved to each of the major issues that concerned the participants. Each person had the opportunity to say their piece and eventually all people took their turn. As the large circle broke up toward evening, each member would take the issues that had been raised and retreat to the campfires, where the ideas would be discussed quietly in small groups. After several days, consensus appeared from the various opinions.

Religious leaders held important roles in these meetings. Although they spoke no more than other members, their opinions had special influence. The group quieted to catch the words as the old man spoke. Each night, the group gathered at his home and sang into the night. This differed markedly from Paraguayan associations in which hierarchy and authoritarian power were the prime organizing factors of political organization.

The regional meetings of the various communities led to a national association of indigenous peoples, the Association de Parcialidades Indígenas (API). API attempted to bring all indigenous groups together to discuss common problems and find solutions.

Despite the optimistic efforts to create API, the agency has had little success in creating a pan-indigenous agency or finding solutions to their problems. In part, the problem stems from the Paraguayan political environment. Paraguay is governed, in many ways, through patronage. People in power distribute goods and favors to loyal followers. The structure leaves little room for popular power and democratic action. Consequently, API finds itself unable to lobby an unresponsive system that is often unsympathetic to its problems.

Secondly, API depends on the sixteen indigenous ethnic groups joining forces as a single entity. Many indigenous groups in Paraguay feel little in common with their pre-Colombian compatriots. When resources become scarce, the coalition of ethnic groups quickly breaks down into dissension and distrust.

A third problem has been that international agencies preferred to give technical aid, rather than promote structural change. The problems of the Guaraní derive from an economic process that is restricting their access to land, placing them on a very few, small reservations. Infusions of medicine, seeds and credit help alleviate some the immediate symptoms of the problem. Disease rates decline, cotton is planted, and new clothes give the appearance of prosperity. But this aid does little to change the long term prospects of the

Guaraní. At the end of each funding cycle, when aid agencies rescind their support and expect indigenous groups to manage on their own, the Guaraní face a critical shortage of land and resources.

In conclusion, recent rapid development in eastern Paraguay has been fundamentally different from previous commercial development. Rather than using a diversity of naturally occurring resources, ranching and agribusinesses target the soil and exploit it intensively. This destroys ecosystems that have adapted to the fragile and thin soil resources of the subtropical regions and kills off the plant and animal species that have thrived there. Ranching and commercial agriculture also destroy indigenous groups. Guaraní groups are restricted to small reservations with only enough land for houselots and small gardens. They have lost the extensive forests necessary for continued hunting and commercial gathering. They are being forced to cultivate cotton and tobacco to get the cash they need for meat and other basic needs. This forces the Guaraní into debt and under the control of merchants, relations that they have avoided throughout two centuries of commercial ties to the larger society.

Assistance to the Guaraní alleviates some of the worst health, economic and social problems of the Guaraní, but it does little to solve underlying problems. The combined wealth and power of international agencies has not solved basic resource problems of the Guaraní nor created political space for democratic action in their behalf.

In summary, Guaraní communities are being destroyed by the economic development of Paraguay's once vast the forests. It is often assumed that indigenous communities are destroyed by contact with other societies, or that indigenous people are trapped in larger commercial systems by their desire to acquire manufactured goods. The case of the Guaraní challenges the contention that integration into commercial systems or contact with the larger society destroys indigenous communities. The Guaraní have been involved with the larger society for generations, even centuries, and it has not destroyed their culture or their social organization. Guaraní have maintained independent communities with distinct ethnic identities, even as they collected forest commodities for sale into international markets. They purchased the goods they needed without becoming inextricably tied to the larger economy.

Guaraní communities are not simply beset by economic development, they are struggling against a particularly destructive type of economic development. Commercial agriculture and ranching demand that the forest be leveled and the soils planted. In essence, intensive development destroys the existing ecosystem and replaces it with a new flora and fauna. The previous ecosystem allowed the Guaraní to maintain diverse production systems, including commercial extraction; new systems force indigenous people to be dependent on a single productive activity. Guaraní were forced to put all of their eggs into one basket.

Where commercial agroforestry allowed the Guaraní independence from the larger society, commercial agriculture forces them to be dependent on merchants and credit. Production credit provides families with necessities until the crop is harvested. These ties to patrons outside Guaraní society undermine the power of traditional religious and kin leaders. The powers of the larger society insinuate themselves into indigenous communities through caciques, who are recognized by the national government. These officials manage relations between the community and the national system. As the national system asserts control over the resources of the community, the new leaders gain power over members of the community.

In closing, it is important to point out that Guaraní society and culture has not disappeared, nor is it likely to do so. First, it is important to note that many Guaraní have maintained their distinct social organization, beliefs and identity, despite four centuries of contact with the Paraguayan state and the international economy. Even today, some Guaraní communities maintain traditional production and social relations in the face of intense pressure from the world system. We should not be hasty in predicting the ultimate of Guaraní society and culture.

Second, the next chapter shows that the Guaraní have lessons to teach the rest of the world. As intensive agriculture and ranching fail in the tropics, developers turn to indigenous peoples for alternate models for development. The Guaraní system of agroforestry not only provides a stable living within the tropical environment, it offers a sustainable profit from the forest.

5

Indigenous Models for Sustainable Development

As conventional development fails in tropical areas, entrepreneurs and environmentalists are looking to indigenous production systems for sustainable means of commercial development. As we learn about the ecological rationality of indigenous groups, these models are being drawn from commercial agroforestry by forest residents.

Agroforestry offers a model for development in lowland forests that is both profitable and sustainable. Although often considered primitive and unprofitable, indigenous harvesting of commercial goods, such as yerba and rubber, can provide greater returns than, rubber plantations, cattle ranches or soybean fields. In fact, recent research shows that the annual profits to be earned from the standing forest outstrip those to be earned from pulp-wood schemes, commercial farming or cattle ranching (Hecht 1992:393).

The world is very aware of the value of timber standing in tropical zones. But most of the value of these forested regions is in non-wood products. In the Peruvian Amazon, the indigenous Bora harvest sixty-one different commodities from the forests, including peach palms, oranges and papaya, which can be sold in the marketplace (Denevan, et al. 1984). Long term returns per hectare from these minor products are greater than from ranching or agriculture (Peters, et al. 1989).

The standing forest not only produces goods this year, but far into the future. The true value of today's forest must include all future production. This figure can be calculated by summing the value of all present and future goods, and adjusting the value of future production to account for interest. This produces a net present value of the forest that includes its future earnings. When the forests are cleared, it destroys the value of that expected profit. The cost of clearing standing forest must be included in models of profits from developing tropical regions. When this ecological destruction is accounted for, the long term profits from sustained harvesting of natural tree crops far surpass the profits from clear cutting.

APPLYING THE INDIGENOUS MODEL FOR RESOURCE USE

Indigenous producers offer models for sustained profits from the natural forest. These production systems have stood the test of time and continue to produce profits. In contrast to the schemes of cattle ranchers and soybean farmers, these indigenous agroforestry systems are small-scale, labor intensive and rely on the existing forest. The following are three projects that build on indigenous agroforestry to shape future economic development in lowland forests.

The Mbaracayú Reserve: Sustainable Development through Mixed Agroforestry

The Guaraní of eastern Paraguay are in a unique situation to demonstrate the sustainability of their mixed economy in the face of destructive development. The Nature Conservancy has recently purchased the land near Ñandurocaí from The World Bank. They intend to protect the forest as a biosphere reserve called *Mbaracayú*. With the help of anthropologists, the Guaraní are being recognized as a critical aspect of this ecological system. If indigenous production activities are included in the reserve management plan, this would preserve the flora and fauna of the reserve, while providing Guaraní commercial profits.

In response to environmental concerns, governments and conservation groups have begun to try to protect areas of existing ocean, savannahs and forests. These have been managed as biosphere reserves, under the aegis of the United Nations Educational, Scientific and Cultural Organization's Man and the Biosphere program (UNESCO-MAB) (Robertson Vernhes 1989). In these self-sustaining areas, development is restricted to protect the natural diversity of the original ecosystems for research and monitoring. One purpose of the UNESCO-MAB biosphere reserve program is to "demonstrate sites of harmonious, longstanding relations between man and the natural environment" (UNESCO 1987). Consequently, biosphere reserves now recognize the importance of indigenous groups who are dislocated by environmental destruction. Since forest peoples manage the so-called "natural" diversity of the flora and fauna, they must be integrated into the design and management of reserves, rather than being treated as artifacts in verdant museums.

The Nature Conservancy, an environmental preservation agency, has undertaken a joint Paraguayan-international effort to protect the ecosystems around Itanaramí. They have purchased the fifty thousand hectare parcel of forest from the World Bank, and are organizing a biosphere reserve on the land. In addition, a zone of influence has been defined that includes the entire Jejuí River basin. A Paraguayan conservation organization, Fundación Moisés Bertoni (FMB), is protecting the existing flora and fauna under the guidelines by the UNESCO-MAB biosphere reserve program. Part of the FMB's plan involves integrating Guaraní yerba collectors into maintenance and development of the region.

There is great potential for sustained yields of yerba from this land. It has historically been Paraguay's highest yerba producing forest, with nine distinct tracts of dense yerba growth. Over each three-year harvesting cycle, the Industrial Paraguaya harvested 250,000 kilos of yerba from these yerbales. At 1993 market rates of over a dollar for each kilo, this comprises an annual income of over eighty thousand dollars.

Four hundred Guaraní families live near the proposed reserve. These five communities, including Itanaramí and Ñandurocaí, have legal title to small tracts suitable for agriculture but insufficient for hunting or commercial gathering on their own land. It is suggested that FMB allow these Guaraní to gather yerba on Mbaracayú land, supplementing the gardens they plant on their own property. Rights to other uses of the biosphere reserve will remain restricted. (The regional population of Guaraní could drastically alter the forest if provided unrestricted trapping or agricultural rights on the land.)

Income from eighty thousand kilos of yerba, even if sold in bulk, would give each family the equivalent of two hundred dollars. With costs of a federation of Guaraní yerba producers removed from that gross, each family would retain several times the present average household income of forty dollars. Some of this profit would offset the adelantados that most patrons advance to workers in the forests. In addition, some of the additional income might capitalize marketing, primarily in trucks for transport. Gathering yerba from the reserve will provide cash to relieve the Guaraní families' needs to clear additional land for cotton production within their communities' forests. This would slow the rate of agricultural clearing and allow fallows time for full recovery.

Commercial gathering on the biosphere reserve could strengthen Guaraní society. Managing resources helps develop the indigenous people's own social organizations. In Mbaracayú, this could be accomplished using indigenous Guaraní institutions. In the past, work teams were formed from the kin networks of the extant communities. These relations form a natural structure that can coordinate the administration of labor and the allocation of profits. In the future, traditional social relations within and between communities might also provide the structure for marketing yerba.

At present, the five Guaraní communities have a loose affiliation, but they lack the formal structure needed for political action or economic cooperation. The production of yerba would not just increase individual households' earnings, it could strengthen this nascent federation of indigenous communities.

Extracting Rubber from the Forest: The Traditional Way

Brazil has been one of the world's largest exporters of natural rubber. Since the arrival of humans in the Amazon, people have used the sticky latex that oozed from the *Hevea brasiliensis* tree in medicines and trapping. At the end of the 19th century, an American by the name of Charles Goodrich developed a process of vulcanization. This transformed the tacky gum into permanent shapes while retaining the material's natural pliability. The discovery created an enormous demand for rubber latex to make tires for the newly invented automobile.

Peasants in the forests organized around the thriving economy of rubber. Rubber tappers, called *seringueiros*, rubber tappers, made shallow cuts into the bark of rubber trees and collected the sap that flowed from the wounds. They sold the latex to merchants who plied the rivers in floating general stores. These frontier families lived in isolated hamlets in the deep forest, largely isolated from the larger Brazilian society. They intermarried with indigenous Brazilians to form a backwoods society of *caboclos*.

The Brazilian latex industry reached its peak in the first two decades of this century. Vast areas of the lowland forests were divided into avenues, of roughly three hundred hectares, where caboclo families searched out and tapped the rubber trees. Merchants arrived periodically with goods, which they sold to caboclos at inflated prices and on credit. Seringueiros were kept in constant debt to these *aviadores*. The Brazilian rubber industry went into decline in the 1920s as latex plantations were cultivated in Malaysia and synthetics garnered a growing portion of the market. As the market slowed, the caboclo population retreated into a mixed economy, depending to a greater extent on hunting, fishing and agriculture to supplement their cash incomes. These traditional extractors also diversified their collecting, selling Brazil nuts (*Bertholletia excelsa*), furs, and other commodities into the international market.

In the 1930s, the Ford Motor Company tried to promote an alternate system of rubber production based on plantation agriculture. The case stands as an argument for the natural production of tree crops. Ford purchased thousands of square miles of the Brazilian rainforest for a rubber plantation called Fordlandia. Ford intended to cover the entire landscape with rubber trees. By densely cultivating the crop, agronomists thought that Ford could raise production and reduce costs. Ford envisioned the entire Amazon Basin covered with cultivated trees, satisfying the growing world demand for cheap rubber tires. The Ford plantation was wiped out by plant diseases that flourished in the dense rubber stands.

As the Brazilian rubber boom ended, seringueiros spent decades in the shadows of the forest, largely forgotten by a nation that was intent on clearing its forests for ranching and agribusiness. Now, as agriculture and ranching fail in the forest, the caboclos are being appreciated for the environmental rationality of their economy. The extractive systems of Brazilian rubber tappers are now viewed as important for protecting the forest while profiting from its existence (Schwartzman 1986).

Rubber tappers caught the attention of the larger world when they resisted ranchers' encroachment into their forests in the 1980s. Bulldozers and logging trucks swept through Brazil's western state of Acre in the 1980s. Many families of tappers in this isolated border region discovered that investors were buying the land and clearing it for ranching. The tappers rose in their own defense. First, they claimed their land under Brazil's tenancy law, which states that a family who occupies a parcel for a year has right to land title. Some seringueiros had lived in the forests for generations. In one famous case, the seringal Cachoeira, tappers blocked construction of a new road onto their land. As media covered the conflict, the seringueiros' struggle was taken up by human rights activists and labor organizers. The struggle became an international issue when one of the foremost organizers, Chico Mendez, was gunned down by killers hired by new landowners. The struggle to guarantee the land rights of tappers of Cachoeira continues.

Tappers are finding a variety of allies in their fight. International environmental groups prefer the sustained commerce of tappers to the destruction wreaked by farmers and ranchers. World Wildlife Fund and Conservation International are working with tappers to establish extractive reserves in the Amazon. Rather than create forests devoid of human inhabitants, these conservation areas include seringueiros as resident managers. In addition, multilateral lending institutions support rural residents in their struggle to protect the environment. The World Bank and The Inter-American Development bank have begun to seek out projects that integrate the extractive reserve model into their own development efforts in lowland forests.

The Brazilian government has responded to the internal and international pressures. In 1987, the Brazilian government passed legislation that recognized the rights of groups of caboclos to control and work land in common. In 1991, the government went farther, reducing the tax incentives for the wholesale destruction of forest for intensive production. Tappers have won provisional recognition of their legal claims and have begun to organize cooperatives to manage their landholdings as reserves. By 1994, eight extractive reserves had been established in the Amazon lowlands. These reserves seek to conserve and manage the forest in the traditional caboclo manner. Residents hunt, fish, garden, and raise domestic animals. As they produce their subsistence, they continue to harvest latex, nuts, and other commodities, as they have done for decades.

Traditional rubber tapping protects the environment and preserves forest managers lifestyles, but it also generates considerable income. The profits won by Brazil's traditional gatherers are impressive. The value of commodities gathered in 1980, alone, was over $70 million (Schwartzman 1986:42). This suggests that since the end of the rubber boom seventy years ago, commodities valued at almost a five billion dollars have been removed from the Amazon. This has provided the Brazilian economy with over a billion dollars in export taxes.

Creating a Demand for Forest Products

The reserves of Mbaracayú and rubber tappers have successfully sought to secure producers' resources. However, there is also a need to create a demand for these forest products, so they continue to generate product. Increasing market demand drives up commodity prices and increases both the profits of indigenous peoples and the value of standing forests.

Plantation production and synthetic materials have reduced the demand for some naturally produced commodities. The demand for yerba mate, for example, is being satisfied by crops cultivated outside the forest. Synthetic materials have supplanted natural rubber, even in the Brazilian market. Two marketing factors impede extractive economies. First, natural forest commodities have difficulty competing with the quantities of scale that other forms of production achieve. Second, forest commodities are generally sold through a vast network of intermediaries who each collect a profit.

Extractive marketing projects directly confront these problems. First, marketing projects create a mass market for goods, inspiring producers to develop the infrastructure to increase production. Second, these projects sell products directly from the forest to manufacturers. This bypasses go-betweens and provides indigenous producers the full value of their goods on the world market.

Since 1986, Cultural Survival has been working to market rainforest products. An early effort of this marketing program focused on Brazil nuts. Brazil nuts have resisted domestication, and the international demand has been satisfied by nuts gathered from Amazonian forests. Caboclos gather nuts in the isolated forests and sell to rural merchants. Merchants, in turn, market the crop to regional warehouses, who sell into the international market. Thus, a nut passed through many hands as it went to market, and each intermediary raised the price and took a profit.

In 1988, Cultural Survival approached the ice cream company, Ben and Jerry's, offering to provide them with Brazil nuts directly from Amazonian gatherers. Cultural Survival used its ties with indigenous groups in Brazil to arrange transport directly from the producer at the farm gate to Ben and Jerry's ice cream plant in Vermont. By not accepting a commission, Cultural Survival assured that profits from gathering went entirely to the families who had collected the nut.

In addition to facilitating the sale of conventional products, groups such as Cultural Survival are searching the forest for new materials to be used in consumer goods. Tropical environments have a vast unexplored flora. The expeditions of biologists return laden with unstudied and unnamed plants. These new forest species yield new products for the world market. Manufacturers analyze these little-known fruits, oils, fibers, and resins, hoping to discover new medicines, foods and beauty aids.

An early marketer of these "green" products was the London-based chain of health and beauty stores, The Body Shop. The Body Shop queried botanists and anthropologists, looking for novel plants to give scent and texture to their products. An array of new plant materials, largely unknown outside tropical forests, found their way into perfumes, bath oils and massage creams. Other corporations have followed the Body Shop's lead, creating an ever-expanding market for new and diverse products from the threatened tropical forests.

Merchants are finding that forest products are highly desirable to an important segment of the consuming public. Many consumers have become educated about the ecological and social problems caused by rampant development in lowland areas. These consumers prefer to purchase goods produced in a nondestructive manner.

Ben and Jerry's Ice Cream quickly discovered that the public was willing to pay a premium for "green" ice cream. By publicizing the sensitive manner in which Brazil nuts were gathered, they could both educate their consumers and explain why they should pay a premium for the product. Moreover, Ben and Jerry's donated a portion of their profits to indigenous peoples and tropical forest preservation. The Body Shop followed suit. Body Shop advertising featured Brazilian indigenous models surrounded by verdant foliage. The imagery emphasized environmental and social sensitivity, while associating the product with what consumers perceived as the healthy naturalness of the forest. The Body Shop also became high profile financial supporters of environmental education and indigenous rights campaigns.

By developing products and streamlining marketing, these projects raise the value of the standing forest. By selling forest goods to an environmentally aware public, marketing projects can return a greater portion of the profits to individuals and groups who will help protect the forest.

Economics as if People Mattered

As Avarijú leaves to cut yerba in the forest, he provides a model for others who hope to win a living from the forest. Agroforestry assures the Guaraní ethnic independence, but it also offers colonists and agribusinesses a model for sustained development. The economy of the Guaraní shows that it is possible to profit from the resources of lowland forests without undermining the viability of the environment.

Indigenous agroforestry provides a model for the long-term development of all lowland forests. Agroforestry provides a means to win profits from the forest without destroying the lowland ecosystem. Annual profits from agroforestry rival those of ranching and agriculture. Although intensive production exhausts resources and undermines future profits, commercial agroforestry allows harvesters to win profits from the forest indefinitely. Indigenous agroforestry protects the ecological diversity of the forest. Ranching and commercial agriculture are destroying flora and fauna that are among the most diverse in the world. In contrast, commercial agroforestry mimics the natural environment and builds on the forest's diversity.

In addition to saving the environment, diversified agroforestry promotes the economic independence and the political organization of producers. Native peoples sell forest products for cash, while they garden, hunt and raise domestic animals for subsistence. The independence of their subsistence sector allows them the economic autonomy to maintain a distinct culture and society. Commercial gathering also requires social infrastructure. Collecting crews need to be organized; bulking centers have to be built; and processing facilities require staffing. Economic independence and social organizing help indigenous groups, as well as other producers, defend themselves against the more powerful national systems that intrude in the forest.

The analysis of agroforestry in Itanaramí shows how ethnic minorities can have direct relations with a national society and the market economy while maintaining their autonomy and independence. Indigenous agroforestry provides the Guaraní a plan for the future. It shows the importance of providing them access to the land and forest for commercial gathering. Just as commercial agriculture and wage labor can weaken social ties, traditional agroforestry can strengthen indigenous social relations.

First, commercial harvesting demands organized groups of laborers. Among the Guaraní, kin groups have organized themselves into collecting crews. Men go into the forest to work with their brothers, cousins and other relations. Rather than being organized by patrons and bosses, work tasks are delegated by consensus. Workers divide profits equally. Thus, rather than undermine traditional Guaraní relations, commercial harvesting strengthens blood and affiliative ties between families.

Second, marketing networks can serve as a template for more extensive federations of indigenous communities. As goods move out of the forest, they flow through various bulking centers. The product of many different work gangs is carried to central bulking stations in the forest, from which that good is carted to central marketing areas. The trade creates a pyramid of links, which brings all the dispersed groups together into a larger organization. In cases such as the Guaraní, where kin-based links between communities are often fluid, trade can help solidify traditional relations, which then serve economic and political functions.

The Guaraní provide a model for future resource use by indigenous people and newcomers to the forest, but the application of this model is not without complexities and possible problems. Extractive production projects must be tailored to the particular conditions and needs of each group.

First, we must not assume that indigenous peoples will choose to continue commercial gathering or even environmentally sound production. Indigenous people might elect to develop commercial agriculture and ranching, production that would destroy the small forests they control. Different lowland groups have different desires for the future. Even within groups, individuals often differ in their hopes and dreams. Should indigenous people decide to develop the forest, it would conflict with environmentalists plans to protect it.

Indigenous people have experimented with intensive agriculture for years, and some will adopt it as a preferred means of making a profit. Some Guaraní will undoubtedly become successful agriculturalists themselves. Families in several Guaraní communities have cleared modest fields for pasture. Cows are kept for milk, oxen for traction, and several families have a few head of beef cattle for profit. In another Guaraní community, residents have felled yerba stands to plant cotton and tobacco. They sacrificed the long term gains of extraction for the short term profits of agriculture, which they hoped would be greater. These efforts to enter the economy of intensive production do not lead to the kind of massive environmental degradation that characterizes large-scale development projects. There are few indigenous peoples and they lack the resources for mechanized clearing. These entrepreurial natives show, however, that the paths of some indigenous peoples will conflict with the desires of environmentalists and the models of anthropologists.

The conflicts that are likely to surface between environmentalists and indigenous peoples are created, to a large extent, by third parties. As private entrepreneurs buy and clear vast areas of the forest, indigenous peoples and environmentalists fight over ever-smaller undeveloped areas. In fact, the total lowland forests managed by environmentalists and indigenous peoples are less than 1 percent of the total region. As indigenous peoples and conservationists attempt to accommodate one another on small parcels, the vast majority of the forests are being destroyed by developers.

A second major problem in using the extractive model to design future development in lowland forests has to do with the social organization of production. Protecting resources and promoting markets builds the potential for a strong extractive economy. However, it is imperative that indigenous residents organize themselves as a group to take advantage of these opportunities. There exists the danger that extractive activities could be controlled by elites outside or within indigenous population.

Most indigenous producers have collected commodities in the forests but depended on nonindigenous merchants and patrons to bulk the product and transport it to market. Few indigenous groups have the regional social networks to organize production for more than their local group. Small and dispersed communities need to create the linkages necessary to move products from the hands of local producers to regional bulking stations and, ultimately, to national and international markets.

In the past, some regional indigenous leaders have taken advantage of the new economic powers permitted by commercial growth, assuming positions of power over their communities and ethnic groups. In essence, these individuals have replicated the mestizo patrons who traditionally controlled marketing. Indigenous caudillos carry the authoritarian relations of rural mestizo society into indigenous communities. In most cases, these Guaraní patrons have been unsuccessful. Community resistance has forced them to relinquish their self-promotion and abandon the power they attempted to assert over others.

The expanding economy presents the opportunity to strengthen existing relations between indigenous individuals and their communities. For example, the Matako of northern Argentina previously gathered timber under the direction of powerful patrons. Today, they have organized themselves as producers' groups based on family connections. Each producers' group provides a representative to a regional marketing board to manage the transport and sale of commodities. With the opportunity of Mbaracayú, the Guaraní could, likewise, transform their loose kin connections into a regional organization for the production and marketing of yerba mate.

CONCLUSIONS

Over the last centuries, the Guaraní of eastern Paraguay have maintained their social organization and distinct culture, despite continual and, at times, intense relations with the larger world. Commercial extraction of yerba mate has provided the Guaraní the means to earn cash without becoming tied to mestizo patrons. Moreover, the extractive activities have provided commercial profit without undermining the forest. By integrating hunting, fishing, gardening and commercial gardening, the Guaraní have diversified their demands on the environment, allowing them to harvest materials without overexploiting any single resource.

The Guaraní are more than an interesting example of ethnic adaptation, their production can help create a model for other groups that live in the forest. Extraction offers indigenous groups and new forest settlers the opportunity to live in the forest and garner profits from its resources. The extractive model offers an environmentally rational method of developing the forest. Profits won through commercial extraction can be greater than those from intensive agriculture and cattle ranching. As the extractive model is being implemented in the lowlands of South America, indigenous groups and forest residents have the opportunity to show the superiority of their production systems in a series of forest reserves.

The final responsibility for saving the forest and its indigenous residents rests with the world community. Will we learn from the lessons we are offered? Can we change our use of tropical resources before the forests are destroyed? It is not simply in the benefit of the forest residents, but for the good of us all.

References

Arens, Richard
1976   Genocide in Paraguay. Philadelphia: Temple University Press.

Baer, Werner and Melissa Birch
1984   Expansion and the Economic Frontier: Paraguayan Growth in the 1970s. World Development 12(8):783-790.

Cabeza de Vaca, Alvar Nuñez
1555/1891 The Commentaries of Alvar Nuñez Cabeza de Vaca, *in* The Conquest of the River Plate. L. Dominguez, ed. London: Hakluyt.

Cadogan, Leon
1959   Como interpretan los Chiripá(Ava Guaraní) la danza ritual. Revista de Antropología 7:65-99.

Chase-Sardi, Miguel
1973   Encuesta Para Detectar la Actitud de la Sociedad Ante el Indígena. Suplemento Antropologico 7(1-2):163-170.

Clay Jason
1988   Indigenous Peoples and Tropical Forests: Models for Land Use and Management from Latin America. Cambridge: Cultural Survival.

Comisión Económica para América Latina y el Caribe (ECLA)
1990   Estudio Económico de América Latina y el Caribe: Paraguay. Santiago: United Nations.

Denevan, Wiliam, et al
1984   Indigenous Agroforestry in the Peruvian Amazon: Bora Indian Management of Swidden Fallows. Interciencia 9(6):346-357.

Fogel, Ramon
1990   Los Impactos de Los Cinco Grandes Proyectos de Desarrollo. Asunción: CERI.

Friedl, Ernestine
1978   Society and Sex Roles. *in* Conformity and Conflict. James Spradley and David McCurdy, eds. pp. 157-167. Boston: Little Brown and Company.

Hecht, Susanna
1992 Valuing Land Uses in Amazonia. *in* Conservation of Neo-Tropical Forests: Working from Traditional Resource Use. Kent Redford and Christine Padoch, eds. pp. 379-400. New York: Columbia University Press.

Hemming, John
1978 Red Gold. Cambridge: Harvard University Press.

Instituto Nacional del Indígena (INDI)
1982 Censo y Estudio de la Población Indígena del Paraguay (1981). Asunción: Instituto Nacional del Indígena.

Kensinger, Kenneth
1984 Marriage Practices in Lowland South America. Illinois Studies in Anthropology: No. 14. Chicago: University of Illinois Press.

Leacock, Eleanor
1972 Introduction. *in* The Origins of The Family, Private Property and the State. Fredrick Engels. New York: International Publishers.

Meliá, Bartomeu
1995 Por qué suicidan los Guaraníes? Accion 154:30-32.

Minge-Klevana, Wanda
1980 Does Labor Time Decrease with Industrialization? Current Anthropology 21(3):279-298.

Nimuendaju, Curt (Unkel)
1914/1978 Los Mitos de Creación y Destrucción del Mundo. Juergen Riester ed. Lima: Centro Amazonico de Antropologia y Aplicación Practica (CAAAP).

Parquet, Reinerio
1985 Las Empresas Transnacionales en la Economia del Paraguay. Unpublished Manuscript prepared for Unidad Conjunta (CEPAL/CET) Buenos Aires.

Pearce, David, Edward Barbier, and Anil Markandya
1990 Sustainable Development: Economics and Environment in the Third World. Brookfield, VT: Gower Publishing.

Peters, C.M., A.H. Gentry, R.O. Mendelsohn
1989 Valuation of the Amazon Rain Forest. Nature 339 (29 June):655-656.

Posey, Darrell et al.
1984 Ethnoecology as Applied Anthropology in Amazonian Development. Human Organization 43(2):95-107.

Redford, Kent, and Christine Padoch
1992 Conservation of Neo-Tropical Forests: Working from Traditional Resource Use. New York: Columbia University Press.

Rehnfeldt, Marilin
1989 Tierra y terror. Los Mbya 3(5):5.

Sahlins, Mashall
   1978   Stone Age Economics. Chicago: Aldine Publishers.

Schor, Juliet
   1991   The Overworked American. New York: Basic Books.

Schwartzman, Stephen
   1986   Seringueiros Defend the Rainforest in Amazonia. Cultural Survival Quarterly 10(2):22-28.

Staden, Hans
   1557/1928 Hans Staden: the true story of his captivity. London: Routledge and Sons.

Turner, R. (ed.)
   1988   Sustainable Environmental Management:Principles and Practice. Boulder: Westview Press.

United Nations Educational and Scientific Organization (UNESCO)
   1987   Report of the Scientific Advisory Panel for Biosphere Reserves. MAB Report Series: No. 61. New York: United Nations.

United States Agency for International Development (USAID)
   1985   Perfil Ambiental del Paraguay. Asuncion:USAID.